AF692349

PIONEERS OF CYBER RESILIENCE

Innovative Approaches in Microsoft Cloud Security and Network

Adesina Abass

© 2021 Adesina Abass

All rights reserved.

No part of this publication may be reproduced, stored in a retrieval system, or transmitted in any form or by any means, electronic, mechanical, photocopying, recording, or otherwise, without the prior written permission of the publisher and author.

Published by: Prodigy Press

Table of contents

Preface iv
Foreword vii
Introduction x

Chapter 1
The New Face of Cyber Resilience in Cloud Driven Enterprises 1
Chapter 2
Understanding Threat Evolution in Microsoft Cloud and Network Environments 13
Chapter 3
Microsoft Azure Security Architecture and Core Defense Principles 21
Chapter 4
Securing Hybrid and Multi Network Cloud Deployments 32
Chapter 5
AI Driven Automation in Threat Detection and Response 40
Chapter 6
Designing Resilient Network Defense Frameworks 49
Chapter 7
Governance, Risk, and Compliance in Cloud Security 57
Chapter 8
Incident Response, Recovery, and Business Continuity in the Cloud 65
Chapter 9
Measuring, Testing, and Continuously Improving Cyber Resilience 78
Chapter 10
The Future of Cloud and Network Cyber Resilience 86

Reviews 93
References 95

Preface

Cyber resilience is often spoken about as a technical capability, but in practice, it is a mindset shaped by experience, discipline, and constant adaptation. As organizations continue to shift critical workloads into cloud environments, the conversation around security has moved beyond prevention alone and into preparedness, recovery, and continuity. This book was written from that understanding. It reflects years of observing how cloud systems behave under pressure and how security decisions made early in architecture design often determine whether an organization withstands disruption or struggles to recover from it.

The Microsoft cloud ecosystem has become a central platform for modern enterprises. Its scale, flexibility, and integration capabilities make it attractive, but these same qualities also introduce complexity. Security teams are no longer defending isolated systems. They are managing interconnected identities, distributed networks, automated workloads, and data flows that cross organizational and geographic boundaries. In such environments, traditional security approaches often prove insufficient. What is required instead is a resilient framework that anticipates failure, adapts to evolving threats, and maintains trust even when systems are challenged.

This book emerged from practical and academic engagement with those realities. It was written to address a recurring gap between theory and implementation in cloud security. While many resources explain individual tools or isolated controls, fewer works connect these elements into a cohesive resilience strategy grounded in Microsoft cloud technologies and modern network defense principles. The aim here is not to prescribe a single solution, but to provide a structured way of thinking about security that aligns architecture, automation, governance, and response into a unified model.

Artificial intelligence plays a central role in this discussion. As threat actors adopt more sophisticated techniques, security operations must operate at a speed and scale that manual processes cannot sustain. AI driven automation offers a way to detect anomalies earlier, reduce operational noise, and respond with greater precision. However, AI is not a substitute for sound design or governance. Its value is maximized only when integrated into well-defined security frameworks that emphasize accountability, visibility, and continuous improvement. This book treats AI as an enabler rather than a shortcut, placing it within the broader context of resilient cloud and network defense.

Another important motivation behind this work is the increasing convergence of compliance and security. Regulatory standards such as ISO 27001 and NIST are often perceived as administrative obligations rather than strategic assets. In reality, when properly implemented, they reinforce resilience by encouraging consistency, documentation, and measurable control effectiveness. Throughout this book, compliance is approached as a practical component of security architecture, especially within Microsoft cloud environments where governance can be embedded directly into operational workflows.

The chapters that follow are intentionally structured to move from foundational concepts to applied strategies. Early sections establish the evolving nature of cyber threats and the architectural principles that support resilience. Later chapters focus on implementation, measurement, and future directions. While the discussion is technical in nature, the language and structure are designed to remain accessible to a broad audience, including security professionals, cloud architects, business leaders, and graduate level readers seeking a deeper understanding of modern cyber defense.

This work also reflects a strong commitment to scholarly rigor. The ideas presented are supported by peer reviewed research, industry standards, and documented practices from the Microsoft security ecosystem. Citations and references are included not only to validate claims, but to encourage further exploration and independent evaluation. Cybersecurity is not a static discipline, and no single publication can offer final answers. What it can do is contribute meaningfully to ongoing dialogue and practice.

Ultimately, this book is written for those responsible for protecting systems that must remain available, trustworthy, and resilient in the face of uncertainty. It acknowledges that breaches and disruptions may still occur, but argues that their impact can be managed and contained through thoughtful design, intelligent automation, and disciplined governance. Cyber resilience is not about eliminating risk entirely. It is about ensuring that when challenges arise, organizations are prepared to respond with clarity and confidence.

It is my hope that this book serves as both a reference and a guide. Whether used to inform architectural decisions, shape governance strategies, or support academic study, it is intended to provide lasting value in a field that continues to evolve. The pursuit of resilient cloud and network security is ongoing, and this work is offered as a contribution to that shared effort.

Foreword

The rapid acceleration of cloud adoption has transformed how organizations build, operate, and secure their digital systems. Microsoft cloud platforms now support critical national infrastructure, financial services, healthcare systems, and enterprise operations across the world. As reliance on these environments deepens, the question facing security leaders is no longer whether attacks will occur, but whether systems are designed to endure and recover when they do. This book speaks directly to that reality.

Cyber resilience has emerged as one of the most important concepts in modern security practice. It requires a shift away from narrow, tool focused thinking toward a broader understanding of how technology, governance, and human decision making interact under pressure. In this context, cloud security and network defense cannot be treated as separate disciplines. They are deeply interconnected, and their effectiveness depends on how well they are aligned within a coherent framework. This work addresses that intersection with clarity and depth.

What distinguishes this book is its deliberate focus on Microsoft cloud environments while maintaining relevance beyond any single platform. The author approaches Microsoft Azure and related technologies not as isolated products, but as components within larger security ecosystems. By grounding technical discussions in real architectural and operational considerations, the book avoids abstraction and instead offers insight that is directly applicable to real world environments.

Equally important is the treatment of artificial intelligence as a practical security capability. AI is often discussed in aspirational terms, yet its real value lies in disciplined application. This work demonstrates how AI driven automation can strengthen detection, response, and governance when embedded within sound security design. Rather than overstating its impact, the book places AI within a balanced framework that emphasizes accountability, transparency, and measurable outcomes.

The integration of governance and compliance throughout the discussion is another notable strength. Many organizations struggle to reconcile regulatory requirements with operational agility. By examining standards such as ISO 27001 and NIST alongside cloud and network security practices, this book shows how compliance can support resilience rather than hinder it. This perspective is particularly valuable for enterprises operating in highly regulated environments.

From an academic standpoint, the book reflects careful research and engagement with peer reviewed literature. Concepts are presented with precision, supported by credible sources, and situated within ongoing scholarly and professional debates. At the same time, the writing remains accessible, making the material useful not only to researchers and graduate students, but also to practitioners responsible for day to day security decisions.

As cyber threats continue to evolve in scale and sophistication, the need for thoughtful, resilient security frameworks becomes increasingly urgent. This book contributes meaningfully to that effort by offering a structured examination of how cloud security, network defense, AI, and governance can be brought together into a cohesive approach. It is a timely and relevant work that will serve as a valuable reference for those seeking to strengthen their understanding and practice of cyber resilience in Microsoft cloud environments.

I commend this book to security professionals, cloud architects, business leaders, and scholars alike. Its insights are grounded, its arguments are well reasoned, and its focus on resilience reflects the direction in which cybersecurity must continue to move.

Introduction

Cloud computing has fundamentally reshaped how organizations design systems, deliver services, and manage information. Microsoft cloud platforms now support a vast range of enterprise functions, from core business applications and data storage to advanced analytics and global collaboration. This widespread adoption has brought undeniable advantages in efficiency, scalability, and innovation. At the same time, it has introduced a new level of exposure. As systems become more distributed and interconnected, the task of securing them becomes more complex and far more consequential.

Security challenges within Microsoft cloud and network environments are no longer confined to isolated vulnerabilities or single points of failure. Modern attacks exploit the very features that make cloud platforms powerful. Identity federation, automated resource provisioning, remote access, and integrated services can all become entry points when misconfigured or insufficiently monitored. Threat actors increasingly rely on persistence, lateral movement, and stealth rather than obvious disruption. These realities demand a security approach that goes beyond traditional perimeter defenses and static controls.

This book is grounded in the concept of cyber resilience as a response to that challenge. Cyber resilience recognizes that absolute prevention is unrealistic in highly dynamic environments. Instead, it emphasizes the ability to anticipate threats, withstand attacks, recover quickly, and continue operating with minimal impact. In Microsoft cloud and network infrastructures, resilience depends on how well security is embedded into architecture, governance, and daily operations rather than treated as an afterthought.

A defining characteristic of resilient cloud security is integration. Microsoft cloud environments combine identity systems, networking, data services, and application layers into a unified ecosystem. Effective defense requires these elements to work together coherently. Isolated tools and fragmented security strategies often create blind spots that attackers exploit. This book explores how integrated design principles can reduce those gaps and support consistent security outcomes across cloud and network boundaries.

Another central focus of this work is the role of artificial intelligence in modern security operations. The scale of data generated by cloud environments makes manual monitoring insufficient. Logs, alerts, and behavioral signals quickly overwhelm even well-resourced teams. AI driven automation provides a way to analyze this information continuously, identify meaningful patterns, and respond to threats with speed and accuracy. However, AI is not presented here as a standalone solution. Its effectiveness depends on strong foundational architecture, clear governance, and alignment with organizational objectives. This book examines AI as a supporting capability that enhances human decision making rather than replacing it.

Governance and compliance are also integral to cyber resilience, particularly in Microsoft cloud deployments used by regulated industries. Standards such as ISO 27001 and NIST are often viewed as compliance exercises focused on documentation and audits. In practice, these frameworks offer structured methods for managing risk, defining accountability, and measuring control effectiveness. When properly implemented, they strengthen resilience by promoting consistency and transparency. This book demonstrates how governance requirements can be embedded into cloud and network security architectures in a way that supports both compliance and operational efficiency.

The scope of this work extends beyond technical configuration. Cyber resilience is influenced by organizational culture, decision making processes, and leadership priorities. Security teams must coordinate with network engineers, cloud architects, risk managers, and business leaders to ensure that resilience goals are understood and supported across the organization. By addressing both technical and strategic considerations, this book aims to bridge gaps that often exist between security design and executive understanding.

The structure of the book reflects this holistic perspective. Early chapters examine the evolving threat landscape and the foundational principles of Microsoft cloud security and network defense. Subsequent chapters focus on architectural design, AI driven automation, and governance frameworks that support resilience at scale. Later sections address incident response, recovery, and measurement, emphasizing the importance of learning and adaptation over time. The final chapter looks toward future developments that will continue to shape cloud security and network defense practices.

This book is written for a broad but connected audience. Cybersecurity practitioners will find detailed discussions of architecture, automation, and defense strategies relevant to real world environments. Cloud and network professionals will gain insight into how security decisions influence system reliability and trust. Business leaders will better understand how resilience supports continuity and long term value. Graduate students and researchers will encounter structured analysis supported by peer reviewed literature and industry standards.

Throughout this work, Microsoft cloud technologies serve as the primary context, but the principles discussed are not limited to a single platform. The focus on resilience, integration, and adaptive defense reflects challenges faced across modern digital infrastructures. By grounding these ideas in practical implementation and academic research, this book seeks to contribute meaningfully to both professional practice and scholarly discussion.

Cyber resilience is not a static achievement. It is an ongoing discipline shaped by evolving threats, technological change, and organizational learning. This book does not claim to offer final answers. Instead, it provides a framework for thinking, designing, and operating secure cloud and network environments that can endure uncertainty. In doing so, it invites readers to view security not as a reactive function, but as a sustained capability essential to modern enterprise success.

Chapter 1

The New Face of Cyber Resilience in Cloud Driven Enterprises

Security failures in modern enterprises rarely begin with a dramatic system collapse. More often, they start quietly with a missed configuration detail, an overlooked access privilege, or an assumption that yesterday's controls will still hold tomorrow. In cloud driven environments, especially those built on Microsoft platforms, these small gaps can expand rapidly, exposing organizations to risks that traditional security models were never designed to handle.

The rise of cloud computing has altered the foundation of enterprise technology. Infrastructure that was once static and physically contained is now elastic, distributed, and deeply interconnected. Microsoft cloud services enable organizations to deploy applications globally, scale resources automatically, and integrate data and identity systems across locations and devices. While these capabilities support innovation and operational efficiency, they also redefine the nature of security. Protection is no longer centered on a fixed perimeter but on dynamic systems that change continuously.

This shift has given rise to the concept of cyber resilience as a core security objective. Cyber resilience goes beyond the idea of preventing attacks at all costs. It recognizes that in complex cloud environments, incidents may still occur despite strong defenses. The focus therefore moves toward minimizing impact, sustaining operations, and recovering quickly without compromising trust or data integrity. For enterprises operating within Microsoft cloud ecosystems, resilience becomes a measure of how well security is embedded into architecture, processes, and governance.

Traditional security strategies were largely designed for predictable environments. Networks were segmented by physical boundaries, users operated within controlled locations, and systems changed slowly. Security controls could be applied uniformly and reviewed periodically. Cloud driven enterprises operate under very different conditions. Resources are provisioned and deprovisioned automatically, workloads span hybrid and remote environments, and identities are no longer tied to a single network or device. In such settings, static security controls struggle to remain effective.

Microsoft cloud platforms reflect this new operational reality. Services such as Azure, Microsoft Entra, and integrated security tooling are built to support scale and flexibility. However, their effectiveness depends on how intentionally they are designed and managed. A resilient security posture does not emerge automatically from adopting cloud services. It is the result of deliberate architectural choices, continuous monitoring, and disciplined governance that align technology with risk management objectives.

At the heart of cyber resilience is the ability to anticipate disruption. In cloud environments, this means understanding how threats target identity systems, application layers, and network connections rather than relying solely on perimeter defenses. Attackers increasingly exploit misconfigured access controls, compromised credentials, and excessive permissions to move laterally within cloud environments. These techniques often evade traditional detection methods because they mimic legitimate behavior. Resilience requires security models that account for this subtlety.

Another defining feature of resilient cloud security is adaptability. Cloud systems evolve constantly as organizations deploy new services, integrate third party tools, and respond to business demands. Security controls must evolve alongside these changes. In Microsoft cloud environments, this adaptability is supported through automation, policy based enforcement, and centralized visibility. When properly implemented, these capabilities allow organizations to adjust security posture in real time rather than relying on delayed manual intervention.

Cyber resilience also depends on visibility. Without clear insight into system activity, risk exposure, and control effectiveness, security teams cannot respond effectively to emerging threats. Cloud driven enterprises generate vast amounts of telemetry data across applications, networks, and user activity. The challenge lies not in collecting this data, but in interpreting it meaningfully. Resilient security frameworks prioritize contextual awareness, enabling teams to distinguish between normal operational behavior and indicators of compromise.

Resilience is equally influenced by organizational mindset. In many enterprises, security is still viewed as a function owned exclusively by technical teams. In cloud environments, this separation is increasingly impractical. Decisions made by developers, architects, and business leaders directly affect security outcomes. A resilient enterprise treats security as a shared responsibility, supported by clear policies, defined roles, and leadership commitment. Microsoft cloud platforms provide the technical tools to enable this collaboration, but cultural alignment remains essential.

The economic dimension of cyber resilience is another factor shaping modern security strategies. Cloud adoption is often driven by cost optimization and operational efficiency. However, security incidents can quickly erode these gains through downtime, regulatory penalties, and reputational damage. Resilient security architectures aim to balance protection with efficiency, ensuring that security controls support business continuity rather than hinder it. This balance is particularly important in large scale Microsoft cloud deployments where resource usage and security investments must be carefully aligned.

One of the most significant changes in cloud security is the growing reliance on automation and intelligence. Manual processes cannot match the speed of cloud operations. As environments expand, the volume of security alerts, configuration changes, and access events increases dramatically. Resilience requires systems that can analyze this information continuously and respond without delay. This is where intelligent automation becomes a critical enabler rather than an optional enhancement.

In Microsoft cloud environments, automation supports resilience through policy enforcement, configuration management, and threat response. Security policies can be applied consistently across resources, reducing the risk of human error. Automated remediation can correct misconfigurations before they are exploited. When integrated effectively, these capabilities shift security from a reactive posture to a proactive one, strengthening the organization's ability to withstand disruption.

Despite these advances, resilience is not achieved through technology alone. Governance plays a central role in ensuring that security practices remain consistent, measurable, and aligned with organizational goals. In cloud driven enterprises, governance frameworks help define acceptable risk, assign accountability, and guide decision making. Microsoft cloud platforms allow governance controls to be embedded directly into operational workflows, supporting continuous compliance and oversight.

The importance of governance becomes even more apparent as organizations face increasing regulatory pressure. Data protection laws, industry standards, and international security frameworks require demonstrable control over information systems. Resilient enterprises treat these requirements as opportunities to strengthen security discipline rather than as administrative burdens. By aligning governance with cloud architecture, organizations can achieve both regulatory compliance and operational resilience.

1.1 From Perimeter Security to Identity Centered Resilience

One of the most significant shifts in cloud driven enterprises is the gradual decline of perimeter based security as a reliable defense model. In traditional environments, security strategies were built around clearly defined boundaries. Firewalls, intrusion detection systems, and network segmentation assumed that anything inside the perimeter was trusted and anything outside was hostile. Microsoft cloud environments challenge this assumption entirely.

Cloud platforms are inherently borderless. Users access systems from different locations, devices, and networks. Applications communicate across services and regions, often without human intervention. In this context, the network perimeter becomes porous and difficult to define.

Cyber resilience therefore begins to move away from network centric trust models toward identity centered security frameworks.

Identity has become the primary control plane in Microsoft cloud environments. Access to resources is determined less by where a user is located and more by who they are, what they are allowed to do, and how their behavior aligns with expected patterns. This shift places identity systems at the core of cyber resilience. When identity controls are weak or poorly governed, attackers can operate freely within cloud environments without triggering traditional alerts.

Resilient enterprises recognize that identity systems must be treated as critical infrastructure. Authentication, authorization, and privilege management are no longer supporting functions. They define the security posture of the entire environment. Microsoft cloud services provide mechanisms such as conditional access, role based access control, and continuous authentication signals that allow organizations to make dynamic trust decisions. These capabilities enable security teams to respond to risk in real time rather than relying on static rules.

An identity centered approach also supports resilience by limiting the blast radius of incidents. When access is tightly scoped and privileges are assigned based on necessity, attackers face greater difficulty moving laterally within the environment. Even if credentials are compromised, the impact can be contained. This containment is a key principle of resilience. It acknowledges that breaches may occur but seeks to prevent them from escalating into systemic failure.

The transition to identity centered security requires more than technical configuration. It demands disciplined governance and continuous oversight. Access rights must be reviewed regularly, automation must enforce policy consistency, and security teams must maintain visibility into how identities are used across cloud and network resources. Without these controls, identity systems can quickly become as vulnerable as the perimeters they replaced.

In cloud driven enterprises, identity centered resilience also influences organizational behavior. Developers, administrators, and business users must understand that access is a privilege tied to responsibility. Clear policies and transparent enforcement help build trust in security processes rather than resistance to them. Microsoft cloud environments offer the tools to support this shift, but success depends on how deliberately they are applied.

Case Study: Strengthening Enterprise Resilience Through Identity Focused Cloud Security

A large enterprise undergoing rapid digital transformation migrated a substantial portion of its operations to Microsoft cloud platforms. The organization adopted cloud services to support remote work, automate internal processes, and scale customer facing applications. While the migration delivered operational benefits, it also exposed weaknesses in the existing security model, which relied heavily on network perimeter controls inherited from on premise infrastructure.

Shortly after migration, security teams observed an increase in suspicious activity that bypassed traditional network defenses. Compromised credentials allowed unauthorized access to cloud resources without triggering perimeter based alerts. Although no major breach occurred, the incidents revealed a fundamental mismatch between the security model and the cloud environment.

In response, the organization initiated a shift toward identity centered resilience. Access to cloud resources was restructured using role based access controls aligned with job functions rather than blanket administrative privileges. Conditional access policies were introduced to evaluate user behavior, device posture, and risk signals before granting access. These changes reduced unnecessary exposure and improved control consistency across the environment.

Automation played a critical role in sustaining this new model. Identity governance processes were integrated into cloud workflows, ensuring that access changes followed defined approval paths and were logged for accountability. Privileged access was time bound and monitored continuously, reducing the risk associated with standing permissions. Security teams gained improved visibility into identity usage patterns, allowing faster detection of anomalies.

The outcome was a measurable improvement in resilience. Attempts to reuse compromised credentials were detected earlier and contained more effectively. Security incidents that previously required manual investigation were resolved through automated policy enforcement. Most importantly, the organization gained confidence in its ability to maintain security despite ongoing changes in cloud workloads and user behavior.

1.2 Embedding Resilience Through Architecture and Design Decisions

Cyber resilience in cloud driven enterprises is shaped long before security incidents occur. It is often determined at the architectural stage, where design decisions either strengthen the environment's ability to absorb disruption or silently introduce long term risk. In Microsoft cloud environments, architecture is not merely a technical blueprint. It defines how identities interact with resources, how networks are segmented, how data flows are controlled, and how failures are isolated.

Resilient architecture begins with the assumption that systems will be tested. This perspective shifts design priorities away from convenience and speed alone toward durability and control. In cloud environments, where services can be provisioned rapidly, there is a temptation to prioritize functionality over structure. When architecture evolves without a resilience mindset, security controls become inconsistent and difficult to manage.

Microsoft cloud platforms provide extensive architectural flexibility, but flexibility without discipline can undermine resilience. Effective cloud architecture emphasizes separation of duties, layered security controls, and intentional segmentation. Workloads are isolated based on sensitivity and function. Network paths are defined clearly, and access is restricted to what is necessary for operation. These decisions reduce complexity and limit the scope of potential compromise.

A resilient architectural approach also acknowledges dependency management. Cloud services rarely operate in isolation. Applications depend on identity providers, storage systems, APIs, and network connectivity. When these dependencies are not mapped and protected, a failure in one component can cascade across the environment. Microsoft cloud architectures that support resilience account for these relationships through redundancy, failover planning, and controlled integration points.

Another important aspect of architectural resilience is consistency. In large environments, security failures often arise from uneven implementation. Some workloads follow best practices while others rely on legacy configurations. Over time, these inconsistencies create blind spots that attackers exploit. Resilient enterprises standardize architectural patterns and enforce them through policy and automation. This approach reduces variability and ensures that security expectations are applied uniformly.

Designing for resilience also means planning for visibility and recovery. Logging, monitoring, and alerting are not afterthoughts. They are built into the architecture from the outset. In Microsoft cloud environments, this involves aligning resource deployment with centralized monitoring and ensuring that recovery mechanisms are tested and documented. When disruptions occur, teams must be able to understand what happened and restore services without unnecessary delay.

Architectural resilience is not static. As organizations adopt new services and expand their cloud footprint, architecture must be revisited and refined. This ongoing evolution requires governance structures that guide design decisions and evaluate risk consistently. When architecture and governance work together, resilience becomes a sustained capability rather than a one time achievement.

Case Study: Designing Resilient Microsoft Cloud Architecture for Enterprise Continuity

A multinational services organization embarked on a large scale migration to Microsoft cloud platforms to modernize its operations and support global growth. Initial deployments focused on speed and functionality, enabling teams to move applications to the cloud quickly. While the transition delivered immediate performance improvements, it also resulted in fragmented architectures with inconsistent security controls across workloads.

Over time, the organization experienced repeated service disruptions caused by configuration errors and unanticipated dependencies. Although these incidents were not always malicious, they highlighted the fragility of the existing architecture. Security teams struggled to isolate issues quickly, and recovery efforts were often reactive rather than planned.

Recognizing these challenges, the organization initiated an architectural redesign centered on resilience. Cloud environments were restructured using standardized architectural patterns aligned with Microsoft security best practices. Workloads were grouped based on sensitivity, and network segmentation was enforced to limit cross environment exposure. Identity and access controls were integrated directly into architectural templates to ensure consistency across deployments.

Redundancy and failover mechanisms were incorporated into critical systems, reducing reliance on single points of failure. Monitoring and logging were centralized, providing security and operations teams with a unified view of system health and activity. These changes allowed teams to identify issues earlier and respond with greater confidence.

The redesigned architecture also improved collaboration between security, infrastructure, and development teams. Clear architectural standards reduced ambiguity and streamlined decision making. Governance processes ensured that new deployments adhered to resilience principles without slowing innovation.

As a result, the organization observed a significant reduction in service disruptions and faster recovery times when incidents occurred. Security events were easier to contain, and operational continuity improved across regions. This case demonstrates how embedding resilience into Microsoft cloud architecture strengthens an enterprise's ability to withstand both cyber threats and operational failures.

By treating architecture as a foundation for resilience rather than a purely technical concern, cloud driven enterprises can build environments that remain reliable under pressure. This architectural discipline complements identity centered security and prepares organizations to integrate more advanced automation and intelligence as their cloud maturity increases.

Chapter 2

Understanding Threat Evolution in Microsoft Cloud and Network Environments

Cyber threats do not evolve in isolation. They adapt in response to how organizations design systems, deploy technology, and enforce security controls. As Microsoft cloud platforms have become central to enterprise operations, attackers have adjusted their methods to exploit the unique characteristics of cloud and networked environments. Understanding this evolution is essential for building security strategies that are resilient rather than reactive.

In traditional enterprise environments, threats were often easier to categorize. Attacks targeted exposed servers, outdated software, or weak network boundaries. Defenses focused on perimeter protection, signature based detection, and periodic patching. While these approaches addressed known risks, they were designed for relatively static infrastructures. Microsoft cloud environments operate under entirely different conditions. Resources are dynamic, identities are decentralized, and workloads shift continuously across regions and services.

Threat actors have learned to exploit this dynamism. Instead of launching obvious attacks that trigger alarms, they increasingly rely on subtle techniques that blend into normal cloud activity. Compromised credentials, abuse of legitimate cloud services, and exploitation of configuration weaknesses have become preferred entry points. These tactics are difficult to detect because they often mimic authorized behavior. In Microsoft cloud environments, where automation and integration are common, malicious actions can appear indistinguishable from routine operations.

One of the most notable changes in threat behavior is the emphasis on identity compromise. Rather than attacking infrastructure directly, attackers target users, administrators, and service accounts. Phishing campaigns, credential harvesting, and token theft are used to gain access without breaching traditional defenses. Once inside, attackers move laterally by exploiting excessive permissions or poorly governed access roles. This approach is particularly effective in cloud environments where identity is the primary gateway to resources.

Network based threats have also evolved alongside cloud adoption. In hybrid environments, attackers exploit the connections between on premise networks and cloud platforms. Weak segmentation, misconfigured gateways, and insufficient monitoring create opportunities for movement across environments. These hybrid attack paths allow threats to persist even when individual components appear secure. Understanding how network and cloud layers interact is therefore critical to effective defense.

Another important aspect of threat evolution is persistence. Modern attackers are less interested in immediate disruption and more focused on maintaining long term access. They establish footholds through backdoor accounts, modified configurations, or abused automation processes. In Microsoft cloud environments, this persistence can be difficult to identify without continuous monitoring and configuration validation. Static security reviews are often insufficient to detect these slow moving threats.

Automation itself has become a double edged sword. While automation enables efficient cloud operations, it can also amplify the impact of security failures. A misconfigured template or overly permissive policy can propagate risk across multiple resources instantly. Attackers understand this and actively look for opportunities to exploit automated workflows. As a result, threat evolution in cloud environments is closely tied to how automation is governed and controlled.

The increasing use of artificial intelligence by threat actors adds another layer of complexity. Automated reconnaissance, adaptive malware, and intelligent evasion techniques allow attacks to adjust in real time. These methods challenge traditional detection models that rely on predefined patterns. Microsoft cloud environments, with their vast data flows and complex interactions, require equally adaptive defensive approaches to counter these emerging threats.

Regulatory and compliance pressures also influence threat behavior. As organizations implement controls to meet standards such as ISO 27001 and NIST, attackers look for gaps created by partial or inconsistent compliance. Controls that exist only on paper or are applied unevenly across environments provide a false sense of security. Threat evolution therefore exploits not just technical weaknesses, but organizational and governance shortcomings as well.

Understanding threat evolution is not about predicting specific attacks. It is about recognizing patterns in how threats adapt to cloud architectures, identity models, and operational practices. In Microsoft cloud and network environments, this understanding enables security teams to anticipate where controls are likely to fail and where resilience must be strengthened. It also highlights the importance of continuous assessment rather than periodic review.

2.1 Cloud Native Misconfigurations as a Persistent Attack Catalyst

One of the most persistent and underestimated sources of risk in Microsoft cloud environments is misconfiguration. Unlike traditional vulnerabilities that often require specialized exploitation techniques, misconfigurations are frequently the result of routine operational decisions. They emerge when services are deployed quickly, defaults are accepted without review, or security settings are adjusted to solve short term problems without considering long term exposure. In cloud driven enterprises, these small decisions accumulate and create conditions that attackers actively seek out.

Microsoft cloud platforms offer a wide range of configurable security controls across identity, networking, storage, and application services. This flexibility is a strength, but it also places responsibility squarely on the organization to apply controls correctly and consistently. Misconfigurations often occur when teams lack a unified understanding of how services interact. For example, a storage service may be secured correctly at the data layer but exposed through overly permissive network access. Similarly, identity roles may be assigned broadly to simplify access, unintentionally granting privileges far beyond what is required.

Threat actors have adapted their techniques to take advantage of these realities. Instead of attempting to breach hardened infrastructure, they scan cloud environments for exposed services and weak configurations that provide legitimate access paths. In many cases, these access paths do not trigger alerts because the services are functioning as configured. This makes misconfiguration driven attacks particularly difficult to detect using traditional security monitoring approaches.

Automation further amplifies the impact of misconfiguration. In Microsoft cloud environments, infrastructure is often deployed using templates and automated pipelines. While this supports consistency and speed, it also means that configuration errors can propagate rapidly. A single misconfigured template can introduce the same weakness across dozens or hundreds of resources. Attackers understand this and focus on identifying patterns that suggest systemic misconfiguration rather than isolated mistakes.

Resilience requires acknowledging that misconfiguration is not a one-time problem that can be solved through initial review alone. Cloud environments change continuously as resources are added, modified, and retired. Security settings that were appropriate at one stage may become insufficient as usage patterns evolve. Resilient organizations implement continuous configuration assessment and enforce baseline policies that align with security and compliance objectives.

Microsoft cloud platforms support this approach through policy driven controls that evaluate resources against defined standards. When integrated effectively, these controls can identify drift from expected configurations and trigger corrective actions automatically. This shifts security from a reactive posture to a preventative one, reducing the time between exposure and remediation. Over time, this discipline significantly limits the opportunity for attackers to exploit configuration weaknesses.

Misconfiguration driven threats also highlight the importance of clear ownership and accountability. In many cloud environments, responsibility for configuration is distributed across multiple teams. Without defined roles and governance structures, security gaps can persist unnoticed. Resilient enterprises establish clear accountability for cloud configuration management and ensure that security considerations are embedded into deployment workflows rather than addressed after the fact.

2.2 Hybrid Network Exposure and the Mechanics of Lateral Threat Movement

Hybrid cloud environments introduce a unique set of challenges that significantly influence threat evolution. By design, hybrid architectures connect on premise networks with Microsoft cloud platforms to enable continuity, scalability, and integration. While this connectivity delivers operational benefits, it also expands the attack surface in ways that are often underestimated.

In many organizations, on premise networks were designed around implicit trust assumptions. Internal traffic was considered safe, and security controls focused primarily on external access points. When these networks are extended into the cloud, those assumptions can persist unintentionally. Attackers exploit this by targeting the weakest point in the interconnected environment rather than the most visible one.

Hybrid connectivity mechanisms such as virtual private networks and dedicated cloud connections create pathways between environments that must be carefully controlled. When segmentation is insufficient, these pathways allow attackers to move laterally from compromised systems into cloud resources or back into on premise networks. This movement often occurs gradually, blending into normal traffic patterns and avoiding detection.

Lateral movement in hybrid environments is particularly challenging because it crosses organizational boundaries. Security teams may monitor cloud activity using one set of tools and on premise networks using another. When visibility is fragmented, attackers can exploit gaps between monitoring systems to maintain persistence. Effective defense requires unified visibility that correlates identity activity, network traffic, and system behavior across environments.

Microsoft cloud platforms provide capabilities to support this level of integration, but they must be implemented intentionally. Network segmentation, least privilege connectivity, and continuous traffic analysis are essential components of resilient hybrid security. Without these measures, hybrid environments can become conduits for attackers rather than enablers of resilience.

Another factor influencing lateral movement is the complexity of hybrid identity systems. When identities are synchronized across environments, compromised credentials can be used to access both cloud and on premise resources. Attackers take advantage of excessive privileges and poorly governed identity lifecycles to expand their reach. Resilient security strategies treat identity as a shared control plane across hybrid environments, enforcing consistent policies regardless of where resources reside.

Hybrid exposure also complicates incident response. When an incident spans cloud and network environments, response teams must coordinate actions across systems with different operational models. Without predefined processes and clear communication channels, containment efforts can be delayed. Resilient organizations plan for these scenarios by aligning response strategies across cloud and network domains and testing them regularly.

Understanding hybrid network exposure is essential to grasping how modern threats evolve. Attackers increasingly view cloud and network environments as a single ecosystem rather than separate targets. By recognizing how lateral movement occurs and how hybrid connectivity can be abused, organizations can design defenses that limit attacker mobility and reduce the impact of compromise.

Together, these threat dimensions reinforce the need for adaptive and integrated security strategies. Misconfiguration and hybrid exposure are not isolated risks. They are systemic challenges that reflect how cloud environments are designed and operated. Addressing them requires continuous assessment, architectural discipline, and governance aligned with the realities of Microsoft cloud and network operations.

Chapter 3

Microsoft Azure Security Architecture and Core Defense Principles

Security within Microsoft Azure environments is not achieved by deploying individual tools or responding to alerts after an incident has occurred. It is shaped primarily by architectural decisions that define how identities are managed, how networks are structured, how data is protected, and how systems are governed over time. In cloud driven enterprises, Azure security architecture serves as the foundation upon which resilience is built, determining whether environments can adapt to pressure or fail under it.

Azure was designed for scale, flexibility, and continuous change. Resources are created dynamically, services are integrated programmatically, and workloads often span multiple regions and operational contexts. This dynamic nature requires a security architecture that assumes constant motion rather than stability. Traditional security models that rely on fixed boundaries and periodic review struggle to remain effective in such environments. Azure security principles therefore emphasize continuous control, real time visibility, and adaptive enforcement.

Identity sits at the center of Azure security architecture. In cloud environments, identity replaces the network perimeter as the primary mechanism for access control. Users, applications, and services authenticate through centralized identity systems that define permissions and conditions for access. This shift reflects a fundamental change in how trust is established. Access decisions are no longer based on physical location or network proximity but on verified identity and contextual signals.

Effective identity security in Azure requires more than authentication alone. Authorization and privilege management are equally critical. Role based access control allows organizations to define what actions identities can perform within specific scopes. When implemented correctly, this approach limits exposure and reduces the impact of compromised credentials. However, role based access is only effective when roles are clearly defined, aligned with operational responsibilities, and reviewed consistently. Excessive permissions remain one of the most common weaknesses in cloud environments, often introduced for convenience and left unaddressed as systems evolve.

Network architecture continues to play an important role in Azure security, even as identity takes precedence. While cloud environments do not rely on traditional perimeters, network segmentation remains essential for controlling traffic flow and limiting lateral movement. Azure supports segmentation through virtual networks, subnets, and traffic control mechanisms that restrict communication between resources. Resilient architectures use segmentation intentionally to isolate workloads based on sensitivity and function rather than relying on broad connectivity that increases risk.

Poorly designed network architecture can undermine even strong identity controls. Flat networks and unrestricted communication paths create opportunities for attackers to move laterally once access is obtained. In contrast, segmented architectures limit the scope of potential compromise and support containment. Azure security architecture encourages a layered approach where identity and network controls reinforce each other rather than operate independently.

Data protection is another core element of Azure security architecture. Data within cloud environments exists in multiple forms and locations, including structured databases, unstructured storage, and transient processing states. Protecting this data requires a combination of access control, encryption, integrity validation, and availability planning. Azure provides native capabilities to support these objectives, but resilience depends on how consistently these capabilities are applied.

Encryption alone does not guarantee data security. Resilient architectures ensure that encryption is paired with strong key management, restricted access, and monitoring of data usage. Backup and recovery strategies are also essential, ensuring that data can be restored quickly in the event of corruption, deletion, or disruption. These measures support not only confidentiality but also continuity, which is a central goal of cyber resilience.

Visibility is the connective tissue that enables all other defense principles to function effectively. Without comprehensive visibility into identity activity, network traffic, and workload behavior, security teams operate with limited awareness of risk. Azure environments generate extensive operational and security telemetry, but the value of this data depends on how it is collected, correlated, and analyzed. Resilient security architectures prioritize centralized monitoring that provides context rather than isolated signals.

Visibility also supports accountability. When security events occur, teams must be able to trace actions back to specific identities, configurations, and decisions. This traceability is essential for incident response, forensic analysis, and governance reporting. Azure security architecture supports this through detailed logging and monitoring capabilities that, when properly configured, offer a clear picture of system behavior over time.

Automation is a defining feature of Azure security architecture and a critical enabler of resilience. Manual processes cannot keep pace with the scale and speed of cloud operations. Azure supports automated policy enforcement, configuration management, and remediation that allow security controls to operate continuously. Automation reduces the likelihood of human error and ensures that security standards are applied consistently across environments.

However, automation must be governed carefully. Poorly designed automated processes can propagate misconfigurations or enforce inappropriate controls at scale. Resilient architectures align automation with clear policies and validation mechanisms that ensure actions are appropriate and reversible. When automation is treated as a controlled capability rather than a shortcut, it strengthens security posture and operational efficiency simultaneously.

Governance provides the structure that sustains Azure security architecture over time. As environments grow and change, governance frameworks define acceptable risk, assign responsibility, and guide decision making. In Azure environments, governance can be embedded directly into deployment and management workflows, supporting continuous compliance rather than periodic assessment. This integration ensures that security principles remain intact even as systems evolve.

Governance also bridges the gap between technical implementation and organizational objectives. Security architecture does not exist in isolation from business priorities. Decisions about access, availability, and protection must align with operational needs and regulatory requirements. Azure security architecture supports this alignment by enabling policy based controls that reflect both technical and organizational considerations.

Case Study: Strengthening Azure Security Architecture Through Identity and Segmentation Redesign

A financial services organization operating across multiple regions adopted Microsoft Azure to modernize its core systems and support rapid service expansion. The migration prioritized scalability and availability, allowing teams to deploy applications quickly and integrate third party services with minimal friction. While the transition improved operational efficiency, it also exposed weaknesses in the underlying security architecture that had not been fully addressed during initial planning.

The organization relied heavily on broad administrative access to simplify cloud operations. Development teams were granted extensive permissions across multiple Azure subscriptions, and network segmentation was minimal to avoid deployment delays. Identity controls existed, but they were loosely governed and rarely reviewed. For a period, this approach appeared to work, as no major incidents were reported and systems remained stable.

Over time, however, security teams began to observe irregular access patterns that were difficult to interpret. Privileged accounts were being used across unrelated workloads, and network traffic flowed freely between environments with different sensitivity levels. Although no confirmed breach had occurred, internal assessments revealed that a single compromised identity could potentially access a large portion of the cloud environment. The architecture lacked the containment necessary to limit impact if an incident were to occur.

In response, the organization initiated a comprehensive redesign of its Azure security architecture with resilience as the primary objective. The first step focused on identity governance. Access permissions were restructured using clearly defined role based access controls aligned with specific job functions. Privileged access was limited to time bound assignments, requiring justification and approval before elevation. This reduced standing privileges and significantly narrowed the scope of potential misuse.

Network segmentation was addressed in parallel. Azure virtual networks were reorganized to isolate workloads based on function and sensitivity. Communication between environments was restricted to explicitly approved paths, and unnecessary connectivity was eliminated. These changes transformed the network from a flat structure into a layered architecture that supported containment and control.

Visibility was also enhanced as part of the redesign. Centralized logging and monitoring were implemented to provide security teams with consistent insight into identity activity and network behavior. This visibility allowed teams to identify anomalies more quickly and understand how different components of the environment interacted. Security events that previously required extensive manual investigation could now be contextualized more efficiently.

The impact of these changes became evident during a subsequent security incident involving compromised user credentials. Although the attacker gained initial access, the redesigned architecture limited movement beyond a small subset of resources. Automated controls detected unusual behavior and revoked access before sensitive systems were reached. What could have escalated into a significant breach was contained quickly with minimal disruption.

Case Study: Enhancing Data Protection and Recovery Through Azure Native Security Controls

A healthcare technology organization managing large volumes of sensitive patient information migrated its data platforms to Microsoft Azure to improve scalability and support advanced analytics. The migration enabled faster data processing and better integration across systems, but it also introduced heightened responsibility for protecting confidential information and ensuring regulatory compliance. Given the critical nature of the data involved, resilience in data protection became a primary concern.

During the early stages of cloud adoption, the organization focused primarily on availability and performance. Data services were secured using default encryption settings, and access controls were applied at a basic level. Backup processes existed but were not standardized across workloads. While these measures met initial operational needs, they did not fully address the risk of data loss, unauthorized access, or prolonged downtime in the event of disruption.

Internal risk assessments revealed gaps in how data was governed and protected across the Azure environment. Encryption keys were managed inconsistently, access to sensitive datasets was broader than necessary, and recovery procedures varied between teams. These inconsistencies created uncertainty around the organization's ability to maintain data integrity and availability under adverse conditions.

To address these challenges, the organization undertook a comprehensive redesign of its Azure data security architecture. The initiative began with a clear classification of data based on sensitivity and regulatory requirements. Access controls were refined to ensure that only authorized roles could interact with specific data sets, and permissions were reviewed regularly to prevent privilege accumulation. This approach reduced unnecessary exposure and strengthened accountability.

Encryption practices were also enhanced. Rather than relying solely on default settings, the organization implemented centralized key management to maintain greater control over encryption processes. This ensured consistent protection across storage and database services and supported compliance with healthcare data protection standards. Key usage and access were monitored continuously, providing visibility into how sensitive data was handled.

Resilience was further strengthened through the standardization of backup and recovery strategies. Backup schedules were aligned with data criticality, and recovery procedures were documented and tested regularly. These measures ensured that data could be restored quickly and accurately in the event of corruption, deletion, or service disruption. The focus shifted from simply backing up data to validating the organization's ability to recover it under realistic conditions.

The benefits of these changes became evident during a service disruption caused by a configuration error in a data processing pipeline. Although the incident temporarily affected data availability, recovery mechanisms functioned as designed. Data integrity was preserved, and services were restored within acceptable timeframes without loss of sensitive information. The organization was able to demonstrate compliance and operational control despite the disruption.

Case Study: Achieving Enterprise Scale Resilience Through Azure Automation and Governance

A large public sector organization adopted Microsoft Azure to modernize legacy systems and improve service delivery across multiple departments. The environment supported diverse workloads ranging from internal administrative platforms to citizen facing applications. While the move to Azure increased operational efficiency, it also introduced governance challenges as teams deployed resources independently using different configurations and security practices.

In the early stages of adoption, security controls were defined but applied inconsistently. Individual teams made configuration decisions based on immediate project needs, leading to variation in access controls, network rules, and monitoring practices. Although no major security incident occurred, internal reviews revealed growing risk. The lack of standardization made it difficult to assess security posture, enforce compliance, or respond quickly to emerging threats.

The organization recognized that resilience at enterprise scale required more than strong architecture at the individual workload level. It required centralized governance and automation capable of enforcing security principles consistently across departments. Without this foundation, even well designed systems could drift over time, weakening the overall security posture.

To address these concerns, the organization implemented a governance driven automation framework within its Azure environment. Security policies were defined centrally to reflect organizational risk tolerance and regulatory requirements. These policies were embedded into deployment workflows, ensuring that new resources complied with security standards from the moment they were created. Non-compliant configurations were flagged automatically and corrected where appropriate.

Automation also played a key role in managing configuration drift. Continuous assessment mechanisms monitored resources for changes that deviated from approved baselines. When deviations were detected, alerts were generated and remediation actions were triggered without manual intervention. This approach reduced reliance on periodic audits and enabled real time enforcement of security controls.

Visibility and reporting were improved through centralized monitoring and governance dashboards. Security and compliance teams gained a consolidated view of access activity, configuration status, and policy adherence across the entire Azure estate. This visibility supported faster decision making and improved collaboration between technical and governance teams.

The effectiveness of the governance framework was tested during a rapid expansion of cloud resources driven by new service initiatives. As teams deployed new workloads under tight timelines, automated policies ensured that security requirements were met without slowing development. Access controls, network segmentation, and logging were applied consistently, reducing the risk of misconfiguration despite increased activity.

Over time, the organization observed measurable improvements in resilience. Security incidents related to configuration errors declined, and response times improved due to clearer accountability and standardized processes. Compliance assessments became more efficient, as evidence of control enforcement was readily available through governance reporting.

Chapter 4

Securing Hybrid and Multi Network Cloud Deployments

Hybrid and multi network cloud deployments rarely emerge from a single, unified design. They are usually the result of gradual transitions, legacy dependencies, regulatory requirements, and operational realities that prevent organizations from moving entirely into the cloud at once. Microsoft cloud environments frequently coexist with on premise data centers, third party platforms, and partner networks. While this model supports flexibility and continuity, it also introduces security challenges that are significantly more complex than those found in standalone cloud deployments.

In hybrid environments, security boundaries are less visible and more difficult to enforce. Traditional assumptions about internal trust often persist from legacy network designs, even as systems become interconnected with cloud services. Attackers exploit this ambiguity. They do not distinguish between cloud and on premise environments. Instead, they look for the weakest link in the combined ecosystem and use it as an entry point to move laterally across networks and platforms.

Securing hybrid deployments begins with acknowledging that connectivity itself is a risk factor. Connections between Microsoft cloud environments and on premise systems are essential for business operations, but they must be treated as controlled interfaces rather than open conduits. Virtual private connections, dedicated links, and network peering arrangements require the same level of scrutiny as external access points. Without intentional design, these connections can provide attackers with unrestricted pathways across environments.

Identity plays a central role in hybrid security. In many deployments, identities are synchronized across cloud and on premise systems to support seamless access. While this improves usability, it also means that a compromised identity can grant access across multiple environments simultaneously. Hybrid security strategies must therefore enforce consistent identity policies regardless of where resources reside. Access decisions should be based on identity, context, and behavior rather than network location.

Network segmentation becomes even more critical in hybrid and multi network deployments. Flat network designs that allow unrestricted communication between environments increase the impact of compromise. In contrast, segmented architectures restrict traffic flows based on function, sensitivity, and trust level. Microsoft cloud networking capabilities support this approach by allowing organizations to define explicit communication paths and enforce restrictions at multiple layers.

Visibility is another defining challenge in hybrid environments. Security teams often rely on separate tools to monitor cloud resources and on premise networks. This fragmented view makes it difficult to detect threats that span environments or to correlate events effectively. Resilient hybrid security requires unified visibility that captures identity activity, network traffic, and system behavior across the entire deployment. Without this integration, attackers can exploit gaps between monitoring domains.

Hybrid deployments also complicate incident response. When an incident occurs, teams must determine where the threat originated, how it moved across environments, and which controls are affected. Without predefined response processes that account for hybrid architecture, containment efforts can be delayed. Securing hybrid environments therefore requires response planning that spans cloud and network domains and assigns clear responsibility across teams.

Multi network cloud deployments introduce additional complexity. Organizations often operate multiple virtual networks to support different business units, regions, or workloads. While this separation can improve organization and scalability, it can also lead to inconsistent security practices if not governed centrally. Security controls applied in one network may be absent or misconfigured in another, creating uneven risk exposure.

Resilient multi network security depends on standardization. Architectural patterns, access controls, and monitoring practices should be consistent across networks unless there is a justified reason for deviation. Microsoft cloud environments support centralized policy enforcement that can apply security standards across multiple networks and subscriptions. This capability is essential for maintaining control as environments scale.

Another challenge in hybrid and multi network deployments is managing third party connectivity. Partners, vendors, and service providers often require access to specific resources. Without strict controls, these external connections can introduce risk. Resilient security strategies limit third party access to defined scopes, enforce strong authentication, and monitor activity continuously. Trust is established through verification rather than assumption.

Cost and performance considerations also influence hybrid security decisions. Organizations may hesitate to implement segmentation or monitoring controls due to perceived impact on performance or expense. However, the cost of insufficient security in hybrid environments often exceeds the investment required for resilience. Security architecture must balance protection with operational efficiency, ensuring that controls support business objectives rather than obstruct them.

Governance plays a critical role in sustaining security across hybrid and multi network deployments. As environments evolve, governance frameworks define acceptable risk, guide architectural decisions, and ensure accountability. Microsoft cloud platforms allow governance controls to be embedded directly into deployment workflows, enabling continuous enforcement rather than retrospective correction.

4.1 Controlling East West Traffic and Redefining Internal Trust in Hybrid Cloud Environments

One of the most persistent weaknesses in hybrid and multi network cloud deployments is the assumption that internal communication can be trusted by default. In many enterprise environments, once traffic is inside a network boundary, it is allowed to move freely between systems. This model originates from legacy infrastructure where internal networks were physically contained and access points were limited. In Microsoft cloud driven environments, however, this assumption no longer holds.

Hybrid deployments introduce continuous interaction between cloud resources, on premise systems, and sometimes third party networks. East west traffic flows constantly between workloads, applications, services, and data stores. When these communication paths are unrestricted, attackers who gain access to any part of the environment can move laterally with minimal resistance. This lateral movement often occurs quietly, avoiding detection because it resembles normal internal operations.

Redefining internal trust begins with recognizing that internal traffic should be governed with the same rigor as external access. In resilient hybrid environments, trust is not granted based on network location alone. Each communication request is evaluated based on identity, function, and necessity. This approach reduces reliance on broad trust zones and replaces them with controlled interaction models.

Microsoft cloud networking capabilities support this shift through granular segmentation and traffic control mechanisms. Virtual networks and subnets allow organizations to isolate workloads based on sensitivity and purpose. Communication between segments is explicitly permitted rather than implicitly allowed. This design limits the number of pathways available to attackers and ensures that access between systems is intentional and auditable.

Controlling east west traffic also enhances detection capabilities. When communication paths are clearly defined, deviations become easier to identify. Unexpected traffic between workloads that do not typically interact can signal potential compromise or misuse. In hybrid environments, correlating traffic data across cloud and on premise networks provides critical context that supports early detection of lateral movement.

Beyond security, redefining internal trust improves operational resilience. Segmented environments reduce dependency chains that can amplify failures. When systems are isolated appropriately, disruptions are contained rather than cascading across the environment. This containment supports faster recovery and reduces the operational impact of both malicious and accidental incidents.

Implementing these controls requires careful planning and collaboration across teams. Network engineers, cloud architects, and security professionals must align on communication requirements and risk tolerance. Without this alignment, segmentation efforts may either be overly restrictive or insufficiently protective. Resilient organizations treat segmentation as an ongoing discipline rather than a one time configuration task.

4.2 Governing Scale, Complexity, and Drift in Multi Network Cloud Deployments

As Microsoft cloud environments grow, they often evolve into collections of interconnected networks supporting diverse functions and regions. Multi network deployments enable scalability and organizational separation, but they also introduce complexity that can undermine security if left unmanaged. Each network may develop its own configurations, access controls, and monitoring practices, creating uneven security posture across the environment.

Configuration drift is a natural outcome of this complexity. Over time, network settings change in response to new requirements, temporary exceptions, or operational pressures. Without continuous oversight, these changes accumulate and deviate from intended standards. Drift is particularly dangerous in multi network environments because it is difficult to detect and often occurs incrementally.

Attackers exploit configuration drift by targeting the weakest segments of an environment. A single permissive network rule or outdated access policy can provide an entry point that bypasses more robust controls elsewhere. Because multi network environments are interconnected, compromise in one segment can lead to broader exposure if segmentation and monitoring are insufficient.

Resilient security strategies address drift through standardization and automation. Rather than managing each network independently, organizations define baseline architectures that apply across environments. These baselines specify acceptable configurations for connectivity, access control, logging, and monitoring. Deviations are tracked continuously and addressed promptly.

Microsoft cloud platforms support centralized governance that enables consistent policy enforcement across networks and subscriptions. Security requirements can be applied automatically when networks are created or modified, reducing reliance on manual intervention. This approach ensures that new environments adhere to established standards from inception rather than requiring retrospective correction.

Managing complexity also requires clear ownership and accountability. In many organizations, network security responsibilities are distributed across teams, leading to fragmented decision making. Resilient environments establish governance structures that define who can approve changes, how exceptions are handled, and how risk is evaluated. This clarity reduces the likelihood of ad hoc decisions that weaken security posture.

Visibility is critical to governing multi network environments effectively. Security teams must have a unified view of network configurations, traffic patterns, and policy compliance across all environments. Fragmented monitoring creates blind spots that attackers exploit. Centralized visibility supports proactive risk management and enables faster response when issues arise.

Complexity also affects incident response and recovery. When networks differ significantly in design and controls, response actions become unpredictable. Standardized architectures simplify response by ensuring that security mechanisms behave consistently across environments. This predictability is essential during high pressure situations where delays or errors can increase impact.

Securing hybrid and multi network cloud deployments requires accepting that complexity is unavoidable while ensuring it remains manageable. Connectivity, scale, and diversity are inherent features of modern cloud environments. Cyber resilience is achieved by imposing structure on this complexity through segmentation, governance, standardization, and continuous oversight.

By redefining internal trust and actively managing configuration drift, organizations strengthen their ability to defend interconnected environments. These measures do not eliminate risk, but they significantly reduce the likelihood that localized issues will escalate into widespread incidents. In Microsoft cloud ecosystems, disciplined management of hybrid and multi network security is a defining factor in sustaining long term resilience.

Chapter 5

AI Driven Automation in Threat Detection and Response

Security teams rarely suffer from a lack of data. In modern Microsoft cloud environments, the challenge is the opposite. Every identity action, network connection, application request, and configuration change generates signals that may or may not indicate risk. As cloud adoption accelerates, this volume grows beyond what human analysts can reasonably interpret in real time. The consequence is delayed detection, alert fatigue, and missed indicators that attackers exploit. AI driven automation emerges in this context not as an optional enhancement, but as a necessary evolution in cloud security operations.

Traditional threat detection relies heavily on predefined rules and known indicators. While these methods remain useful for identifying familiar attack patterns, they struggle to keep pace with adaptive threats that blend into normal cloud activity. In Microsoft cloud environments, where automation and integration are fundamental features, malicious behavior often mirrors legitimate operations. Attackers use valid credentials, authorized services, and approved interfaces to avoid detection. AI driven approaches address this challenge by focusing on behavior rather than signatures.

At its core, AI driven threat detection seeks to understand what normal looks like within a given environment. By analyzing historical activity across identities, workloads, and networks, machine learning models establish behavioral baselines. Deviations from these baselines signal potential risk, even when no known attack pattern is present. This capability is particularly valuable in cloud environments, where variability is expected but still measurable over time.

AI driven automation also transforms how alerts are generated and prioritized. In traditional models, security teams are often overwhelmed by high volumes of low value alerts. Many of these alerts represent benign activity or misconfigurations rather than genuine threats. By applying contextual analysis, AI systems can correlate signals across multiple data sources and reduce false positives. This allows analysts to focus their attention on events that pose real risk rather than reacting to noise.

Response is another area where automation significantly enhances resilience. Manual response processes are often too slow to contain fast moving cloud threats. Once attackers gain access, they can modify configurations, create new resources, or exfiltrate data within minutes. Automated response mechanisms enable organizations to act immediately when risk thresholds are exceeded. Actions such as revoking access, isolating workloads, or enforcing stricter controls can occur without waiting for human intervention.

In Microsoft cloud environments, AI driven automation supports this rapid response by integrating detection with enforcement. When anomalous behavior is identified, automated workflows can trigger predefined actions aligned with governance policies. This integration ensures that response actions are consistent, auditable, and aligned with organizational risk tolerance. Automation does not replace human oversight, but it extends the reach of security teams and buys critical time during incidents.

Another important contribution of AI driven automation is its ability to adapt over time. As environments evolve, machine learning models refine their understanding of normal behavior. This adaptability is essential in cloud deployments where workloads, users, and configurations change frequently. Static detection rules often require constant tuning to remain effective. AI driven systems reduce this burden by learning continuously from new data and adjusting detection logic accordingly.

However, effective use of AI in threat detection and response requires disciplined implementation. Poorly trained models or insufficient context can lead to inaccurate conclusions and unintended consequences. Resilient organizations treat AI as part of a broader security framework rather than a standalone solution. Human expertise remains essential for validating insights, refining response strategies, and ensuring ethical and operational oversight.

Governance also plays a critical role in AI driven automation. Automated response actions must align with defined policies and compliance requirements. For example, isolating a workload may be appropriate in one context but disruptive in another. Clear governance ensures that automation operates within acceptable boundaries and that decisions can be reviewed and explained. In Microsoft cloud environments, governance controls can be embedded into automation workflows to support accountability and transparency.

AI driven automation further supports resilience by improving consistency. Human decision making varies under pressure, especially during complex incidents. Automated processes execute responses reliably and repeatably, reducing the risk of error. This consistency is particularly valuable in large scale cloud environments where manual coordination across teams and regions can introduce delays.

Despite its advantages, AI driven automation is not a shortcut to security maturity. It amplifies both strengths and weaknesses in underlying architecture. Poor identity governance, weak segmentation, or inconsistent logging limit the effectiveness of AI systems. Resilient cloud security strategies therefore prioritize foundational controls before relying on advanced automation. When these foundations are in place, AI becomes a powerful force multiplier.

5.1 Behavioral Analytics and Context Aware Threat Identification in Cloud Environments

In Microsoft cloud environments, the line between legitimate activity and malicious behavior is often difficult to define. Cloud systems are designed to be dynamic. Users log in from different locations, services scale automatically, and applications communicate continuously across resources. Traditional security detection methods, which rely on fixed rules or known attack signatures, struggle to operate effectively in this level of variability. Behavioral analytics addresses this limitation by shifting the focus from what attackers use to how activity unfolds over time.

Behavioral analytics relies on machine learning models that study historical activity to establish patterns of normal behavior. These patterns are not limited to users alone. They include service accounts, application workflows, network communication paths, and administrative actions. In Microsoft cloud environments, this analysis spans identity usage, resource access frequency, configuration changes, and interaction between services. By understanding these baselines, AI systems are able to detect subtle deviations that would otherwise go unnoticed.

What makes behavioral analytics particularly valuable is its ability to detect threats that do not rely on malware or obvious exploitation. Many modern attacks begin with valid credentials obtained through phishing or credential reuse. When attackers authenticate successfully, traditional defenses may see no immediate issue. Behavioral analytics examines how those credentials are used. Unusual access sequences, abnormal resource targeting, or activity outside established behavioral patterns can indicate compromise even when authentication appears legitimate.

Context plays a critical role in strengthening detection accuracy. A single anomaly rarely provides enough information to justify a response. AI driven systems improve confidence by correlating multiple signals. For example, an identity accessing unfamiliar resources may be benign in isolation. When combined with network movement, privilege escalation attempts, or configuration changes, the risk profile changes significantly. Context aware detection allows security teams to focus on meaningful threats rather than isolated events.

Behavioral analytics also adapts to change. Cloud environments evolve constantly as organizations deploy new services, onboard users, and modify workflows. Static detection rules often require frequent tuning to remain effective. Machine learning models update their understanding of normal behavior as environments change, reducing false positives while maintaining sensitivity to genuine threats. This adaptability is essential for maintaining resilience in cloud deployments where change is continuous.

Despite its advantages, behavioral analytics must be implemented with care. Poor data quality, incomplete visibility, or insufficient context can undermine effectiveness. Resilient organizations ensure that logging, monitoring, and identity governance are robust before relying heavily on AI driven detection. When these foundations are in place, behavioral analytics becomes a powerful capability that significantly improves early threat identification and reduces the dwell time of attackers within Microsoft cloud environments.

5.2 Automating Threat Response While Preserving Governance and Oversight

Detection alone is insufficient in modern cloud security. Once a threat is identified, the speed and consistency of response determine whether impact is contained or escalates. In Microsoft cloud environments, attackers can act quickly, modifying configurations, creating new resources, or exfiltrating data within minutes. Manual response processes are often too slow to keep pace with this speed. AI driven automation addresses this gap by enabling immediate, policy aligned response actions.

Automated response workflows execute predefined actions when specific risk thresholds are reached. These actions may include revoking access credentials, restricting network communication, isolating affected workloads, or enforcing stricter identity controls. By embedding these responses into automated systems, organizations reduce reliance on human availability during critical moments. Automation ensures that containment actions occur consistently regardless of time, workload, or staffing conditions.

However, automation introduces its own risks if not governed carefully. Overly aggressive responses can disrupt legitimate business operations, while insufficient responses may fail to contain threats. Resilient automation frameworks balance speed with control by applying graduated response strategies. Not every anomaly requires immediate isolation. Some events may warrant monitoring, others investigation, and only the most severe demand automatic containment. Clear classification and response logic are essential to maintaining this balance.

Governance ensures that automated responses align with organizational risk tolerance and regulatory obligations. In Microsoft cloud environments, governance controls define which actions automation is allowed to take and under what circumstances. These controls ensure that responses are auditable, explainable, and consistent with compliance requirements. Automation operates within defined boundaries rather than making uncontrolled decisions.

Human oversight remains essential even in highly automated environments. Security teams review automated actions, assess outcomes, and refine response strategies based on experience. This feedback loop strengthens automation over time, ensuring that it remains aligned with evolving threats and operational realities. Automation handles execution at speed, while humans provide judgment, accountability, and strategic direction.

When implemented correctly, automated response enhances resilience by reducing reaction time and minimizing impact. It does not replace human expertise. Instead, it allows security teams to focus on investigation, improvement, and strategic planning while automation handles repetitive and time sensitive actions. In cloud environments where speed is a defining factor, this combination of automation and oversight is critical to effective defense.

5.3 Scaling Security Operations Through Intelligent and Adaptive Automation

As Microsoft cloud environments expand, security operations must scale accordingly. The volume of alerts, logs, and configuration changes generated by cloud systems can overwhelm even well resourced teams. Without intelligent automation, security operations become reactive, focusing on alert triage rather than risk reduction. AI driven automation provides a way to scale security capabilities without proportional increases in personnel.

Intelligent automation improves scalability by prioritizing information rather than simply processing it. AI systems analyze incoming signals and group related events into coherent incidents. This reduces noise and presents security analysts with a manageable number of meaningful cases rather than thousands of isolated alerts. By focusing attention where it matters most, automation improves efficiency and reduces fatigue.

Automation also supports consistency across large and distributed environments. In many organizations, different teams respond differently to similar incidents, leading to uneven outcomes. Automated workflows ensure that response actions follow defined standards regardless of where incidents occur. This consistency supports better documentation, easier auditing, and more predictable results during incidents.

Adaptive automation further strengthens resilience by learning from experience. Each incident provides data that can be used to refine detection models and response logic. Over time, automation becomes more accurate and effective, reflecting the unique characteristics of the environment it protects. This continuous learning process is essential in cloud environments where threats and operations evolve rapidly.

Scalability is not solely about handling volume. It is also about maintaining quality. Automation enables security teams to maintain high standards of response even as environments grow. Routine tasks are handled automatically, freeing analysts to focus on complex investigations, architectural improvements, and governance activities. This shift improves both effectiveness and job sustainability for security professionals.

Ultimately, intelligent automation transforms security operations from a reactive function into a proactive capability. By combining behavioral analytics, governed response, and adaptive learning, organizations build security programs that scale with their Microsoft cloud environments. This scalability is a defining characteristic of cyber resilience, ensuring that security remains effective even as complexity increases.

Chapter 6

Designing Resilient Network Defense Frameworks

Network defense has long been a foundational element of cybersecurity, yet its role has changed significantly in cloud driven enterprises. In traditional environments, network security focused on protecting fixed boundaries through firewalls, intrusion prevention systems, and tightly controlled access points. Microsoft cloud environments have reshaped this model. Networks are now software defined, distributed, and deeply integrated with identity and application layers. Designing resilient network defense frameworks requires a shift in thinking from static protection to adaptive control.

In modern cloud architectures, networks are no longer isolated conduits for data. They actively influence how systems communicate, how threats propagate, and how incidents are contained. In Microsoft cloud environments, network defense must account for hybrid connectivity, dynamic workloads, and continuous change. Resilience depends on the ability of network controls to adapt to evolving conditions without introducing fragility or excessive complexity.

A resilient network defense framework begins with clarity of purpose. Networks exist to enable communication between systems, users, and services. Security controls should support this purpose rather than obstruct it. Overly restrictive designs can impede operations, while overly permissive ones increase risk. Effective network defense balances accessibility with control, ensuring that communication occurs only where it is necessary and justified.

Segmentation is a central principle in resilient network design. By dividing networks into logical segments based on function, sensitivity, and trust level, organizations limit the potential impact of compromise. In Microsoft cloud environments, segmentation is achieved through virtual networks, subnets, and traffic control mechanisms that restrict communication paths. When segmentation is applied consistently, it reduces lateral movement and supports containment.

Resilient network frameworks also prioritize visibility. Without insight into traffic flows and communication patterns, security teams operate reactively. Modern network defense requires continuous monitoring that captures both permitted and denied traffic, providing context for security decisions. In hybrid deployments, visibility must span cloud and on premise environments to ensure a unified understanding of risk.

Identity integration further strengthens network defense. Rather than relying solely on network location, resilient frameworks incorporate identity signals into access decisions. This approach aligns network security with modern cloud identity models and reduces reliance on implicit trust. Communication between systems is governed by who or what is requesting access and why, not just where the request originates.

Automation plays an increasingly important role in network defense. As environments scale, manual management of network rules becomes impractical. Automated enforcement ensures that segmentation, access controls, and monitoring are applied consistently. When combined with governance, automation supports continuous alignment with security objectives even as networks evolve.

Resilient network defense frameworks also account for failure. Networks are designed to support redundancy, fault tolerance, and rapid recovery. When disruptions occur, systems should degrade gracefully rather than collapse. This resilience supports both security and availability, ensuring that network defenses do not become single points of failure.

Governance provides the structure that sustains network defense over time. Clear policies define acceptable communication patterns, guide design decisions, and assign accountability. In Microsoft cloud environments, governance controls can be embedded into network management workflows, supporting continuous enforcement and compliance.

6.1 Segmenting Networks to Contain Threat Propagation

One of the most critical yet frequently misunderstood elements of resilient network defense is segmentation. In cloud driven enterprises, segmentation is not simply a way to organize resources. It is a deliberate security strategy designed to control how threats move through an environment. In Microsoft cloud ecosystems, where workloads communicate dynamically and scale automatically, segmentation determines whether an incident remains localized or spreads rapidly across systems.

Traditional network designs often favored broad connectivity for ease of management. Systems within the same network could communicate freely, and restrictions were applied primarily at the perimeter. While this approach simplified operations, it also created expansive trust zones. Once attackers breached the perimeter, they encountered few obstacles to lateral movement. In cloud environments, this weakness is amplified by automation and scale.

Resilient network defense frameworks reject the assumption that internal communication should be unrestricted. Instead, they define explicit trust boundaries based on workload function, data sensitivity, and operational role. Segmentation ensures that systems communicate only when there is a clear and justified requirement. This approach significantly reduces the number of pathways available to attackers and limits the impact of compromise.

Microsoft cloud networking capabilities support fine grained segmentation through virtual networks, subnets, and controlled routing. Workloads can be isolated by environment, such as production and development, or by business function, such as finance and operations. Communication between these segments is governed by clearly defined rules rather than implicit trust. This structure enables security teams to reason about network behavior and enforce consistent controls.

Segmentation also enhances detection and response. When communication paths are limited and well defined, unexpected traffic becomes more visible. Anomalous connections between segments that rarely interact can indicate potential compromise. This clarity supports faster investigation and more confident response decisions. In contrast, flat networks generate so much internal traffic that meaningful signals are easily lost.

Effective segmentation requires coordination between network design and operational needs. Over segmentation can introduce complexity that hinders performance and maintainability. Under segmentation leaves environments exposed. Resilient frameworks strike a balance by aligning segmentation decisions with risk assessments and business priorities. Microsoft cloud environments provide the flexibility to adjust segmentation as requirements evolve, supporting continuous improvement rather than rigid design.

Segmentation is not a one-time task. As new workloads are deployed and integrations change, network boundaries must be reviewed and updated. Governance and automation play essential roles in sustaining segmentation over time. Without these mechanisms, environments gradually drift back toward permissive connectivity, eroding resilience.

Case Study: Limiting Lateral Movement Through Strategic Network Segmentation

A regional telecommunications company migrated its customer management and billing systems to Microsoft cloud platforms to improve scalability and service reliability. The initial network design emphasized simplicity and performance. All core workloads were deployed within a small number of virtual networks with broad internal connectivity. While this approach supported rapid deployment, it also created large trust zones with minimal internal restrictions.

During a routine security assessment, the organization identified that a compromised application server could potentially access multiple sensitive systems, including customer data stores and administrative services. Although no breach had occurred, the assessment revealed that the existing network architecture lacked effective containment mechanisms. A single point of compromise could escalate into a widespread incident.

In response, the organization redesigned its network architecture around segmentation principles. Workloads were grouped into distinct network segments based on function and sensitivity. Customer facing applications were separated from backend processing systems, and administrative services were isolated into restricted segments. Communication between segments was permitted only through defined pathways aligned with application requirements.

Network rules were documented and reviewed to ensure they reflected operational needs rather than convenience. Unused connectivity paths were eliminated, reducing the overall attack surface. Monitoring was enhanced to track traffic between segments and detect deviations from expected patterns. These changes transformed the network from a flat environment into a layered defense structure.

The effectiveness of the redesign was demonstrated during a subsequent incident involving a compromised web application component. Although the attacker gained initial access, network segmentation prevented movement beyond the affected segment. Attempts to connect to backend systems were blocked, and security teams were alerted to the unusual traffic. The incident was contained quickly without impact to critical systems or customer data.

6.2 Integrating Network Defense With Identity and Context Signals

Resilient network defense frameworks can no longer rely on network location as the primary indicator of trust. In Microsoft cloud environments, users, applications, and services operate across distributed networks, devices, and regions. A request originating from an internal network segment does not automatically imply legitimacy. As a result, modern network defense must integrate identity and contextual signals into decision making processes to remain effective.

Traditional network security models often treated identity and network controls as separate layers. Firewalls and routing rules governed traffic flow, while identity systems managed authentication and authorization. In cloud driven enterprises, this separation creates gaps that attackers exploit. When identities are compromised, network controls that rely solely on location provide little resistance. Integrating identity awareness into network defense closes this gap and strengthens resilience.

Identity integrated network defense evaluates who or what is requesting access, the context of the request, and the risk associated with the activity. Contextual factors may include device posture, authentication strength, behavioral patterns, and sensitivity of the target resource. By incorporating these signals, network defenses can make more informed decisions about whether to allow, restrict, or monitor communication.

Microsoft cloud environments support this integration by enabling network controls to reference identity and policy context. Access between systems is no longer governed only by static network rules. Instead, it is influenced by dynamic conditions that reflect real time risk. This approach reduces reliance on implicit trust and ensures that network access adapts to changing threat conditions.

Integrating identity and context also improves containment. When suspicious behavior is detected, network controls can respond by restricting communication associated with specific identities or workloads rather than disabling entire network segments. This precision minimizes disruption while maintaining security. It also supports faster response by narrowing the scope of investigation and remediation.

Another benefit of identity integrated network defense is improved visibility. By correlating network activity with identity actions, security teams gain a clearer understanding of how threats unfold across environments. This correlation supports more accurate incident analysis and reduces uncertainty during response efforts. Without identity context, network alerts often lack sufficient detail to guide effective action.

Implementing this integration requires careful planning and governance. Identity signals must be reliable, and policies must reflect organizational risk tolerance. Overly strict controls can disrupt legitimate operations, while overly permissive ones undermine security. Resilient organizations iterate on policy design, refining controls based on operational feedback and evolving threats.

As cloud environments continue to grow in complexity, integrating identity and context into network defense becomes essential. It aligns network security with modern cloud realities and supports adaptive response. This integration transforms network defense from a static barrier into a dynamic control system capable of responding to real time risk.

Chapter 7

Governance, Risk, and Compliance in Cloud Security

Security in cloud environments does not fail solely because of weak technology. More often, it fails because decisions are made without structure, risks are accepted implicitly rather than deliberately, and accountability is unclear. In Microsoft cloud environments, where resources are created and modified rapidly, governance becomes the framework that ensures security remains intentional rather than accidental. Governance, risk, and compliance are therefore not supporting functions. They are core components of cyber resilience.

The nature of cloud computing fundamentally changes how organizations must think about control. Traditional governance models were built for environments where systems were relatively static and changes followed long approval cycles. Cloud environments operate differently. Infrastructure can be deployed in minutes, access can be granted instantly, and configurations can change continuously through automation. Without governance adapted to this reality, organizations lose visibility and control over their security posture.

Governance in Microsoft cloud environments begins with defining clear expectations. These expectations include what types of resources are allowed, how they should be configured, who can create or modify them, and how risk decisions are made. When expectations are vague or undocumented, teams rely on assumptions that vary widely across the organization. This inconsistency creates gaps that attackers exploit and makes incident response more difficult.

Risk management is closely tied to governance, but it requires a different mindset in cloud environments. Risk is not a static condition that can be assessed once and revisited annually. It is dynamic, influenced by changes in architecture, identity usage, third party integrations, and threat activity. In Microsoft cloud deployments, risk must be monitored continuously and addressed proactively. This requires visibility into configurations, access patterns, and control effectiveness across environments.

Effective cloud risk management recognizes that not all risks can or should be eliminated. Instead, risks must be identified, evaluated, and accepted deliberately. Governance frameworks define who has the authority to accept risk and under what conditions. This clarity prevents unmanaged exposure and ensures that risk decisions align with organizational priorities rather than convenience or urgency.

Compliance frameworks provide structure to this process. Standards such as ISO 27001 and NIST are often perceived as compliance checklists disconnected from operational realities. In resilient cloud environments, these frameworks are treated as design guides rather than audit requirements. They define principles for access control, monitoring, incident response, and governance that support both security and accountability.

When compliance is integrated into Microsoft cloud architecture, it becomes part of daily operations. Policies enforce configuration standards automatically. Access controls reflect documented roles and responsibilities. Logging and monitoring generate evidence continuously rather than during audit periods. This integration reduces the friction typically associated with compliance and strengthens security posture at the same time.

A common challenge in cloud governance is balancing control with agility. Development teams need freedom to innovate, deploy, and experiment. Excessive restriction can slow progress and encourage workarounds that introduce risk. Resilient governance frameworks focus on guardrails rather than gates. They define safe boundaries within which teams can operate confidently, knowing that security expectations are clear and enforced consistently.

Automation is essential to achieving this balance. Manual governance processes cannot keep pace with the speed of cloud operations. Policy driven enforcement ensures that standards are applied automatically whenever resources are created or modified. This reduces reliance on human intervention and prevents configuration drift. In Microsoft cloud environments, automation allows governance to scale alongside infrastructure growth.

Accountability is another pillar of effective governance. Cloud environments distribute responsibility across multiple roles and teams. Developers configure applications, administrators manage access, security teams define policies, and business leaders accept risk. Without clear accountability, issues fall between roles and remain unresolved.

Governance frameworks clarify ownership and decision making authority, ensuring that security responsibilities are understood and enforced.

Visibility underpins all governance, risk, and compliance efforts. Organizations cannot govern what they cannot see. Microsoft cloud platforms generate extensive telemetry that provides insight into resource configurations, identity usage, and policy compliance. Resilient governance frameworks consolidate this information into dashboards and reports that support oversight and informed decision making at both technical and executive levels.

Incident response and recovery are also influenced by governance. When an incident occurs, teams must know who is authorized to act, what actions are permitted, and how decisions should be documented. Governance frameworks provide this clarity, reducing confusion during high pressure situations. Clear processes and accountability improve response speed and reduce the likelihood of errors that exacerbate impact.

Compliance additionally plays a role in building external trust. Customers, partners, and regulators increasingly expect organizations to demonstrate control over cloud environments. Evidence of compliance signals maturity and reliability. When compliance is embedded into operations rather than treated as an afterthought, organizations are better positioned to meet these expectations without disrupting business activities.

Over time, governance frameworks must evolve alongside cloud environments. New services, threat models, and regulatory requirements require ongoing refinement of policies and controls. Resilient organizations treat governance as a continuous discipline rather than a static program. Regular review and improvement ensure that governance remains aligned with both security objectives and operational realities.

7.1 Embedding Governance Into Cloud Architecture and Daily Operations

One of the most common reasons cloud governance fails is because it exists only as documentation rather than as an operational capability. Policies may be clearly written, risk registers carefully maintained, and compliance requirements well understood, yet none of these translate into consistent behavior across cloud environments. In Microsoft cloud deployments, resilient governance is achieved only when it is embedded directly into architecture and daily operational workflows.

Embedding governance into cloud architecture begins with designing environments that reflect organizational rules by default. Instead of relying on teams to remember policies, architectures are structured so that secure and compliant behavior is the easiest path. Network segmentation, access boundaries, and resource organization are defined centrally and inherited by workloads automatically. This approach reduces the likelihood of accidental noncompliance and ensures that security expectations are enforced consistently.

Microsoft cloud platforms support this architectural embedding through centralized management and policy enforcement capabilities. Governance controls can restrict which services may be deployed, how they must be configured, and where sensitive data may reside. When these controls are integrated into deployment pipelines, governance becomes part of the build process rather than a post deployment correction. This integration shifts governance from reactive oversight to proactive control.

Daily operations also play a critical role in sustaining governance. Access requests, configuration changes, and exception handling must follow defined processes that reflect risk tolerance and accountability. When operational workflows bypass governance controls, risk accumulates quietly. Resilient organizations align operational processes with governance frameworks, ensuring that changes are reviewed, documented, and auditable without introducing unnecessary delay.

Another important aspect of operational governance is education and alignment. Teams must understand not only what rules exist but why they matter. When governance is perceived as arbitrary, compliance becomes superficial. When it is linked to resilience and operational stability, it gains broader support. Clear communication and ongoing engagement help embed governance into organizational culture as well as technical systems.

Embedding governance into architecture and operations transforms security from an external constraint into an internal capability. It ensures that as cloud environments evolve, governance remains intact and effective. This integration is essential for maintaining resilience in Microsoft cloud deployments where change is constant and complexity grows over time.

7.2 Managing Third Party and Supply Chain Risk in Cloud Ecosystems

Cloud environments rarely operate in isolation. Modern enterprises depend on third party services, vendors, and partners that integrate directly with Microsoft cloud platforms. These relationships introduce additional risk that extends beyond internal controls. Supply chain and third party risk has become a significant factor in cloud security, as attackers increasingly target indirect access paths to bypass hardened environments.

Managing third party risk begins with visibility. Organizations must understand which external entities have access to cloud resources, what level of access they hold, and how that access is governed. In Microsoft cloud environments, third party integrations may involve application permissions, API access, or shared network connectivity. Without clear oversight, these integrations can create hidden attack surfaces.

Governance frameworks define how third party access is granted, reviewed, and revoked. Access should be limited to specific scopes aligned with contractual and operational requirements. Excessive or indefinite access increases risk and reduces accountability. Resilient organizations implement periodic reviews to ensure that third party permissions remain necessary and appropriate.

Supply chain risk also extends to software and services deployed within cloud environments. Dependencies introduced through external libraries, managed services, or automation tools can affect security posture. Governance frameworks require due diligence before adoption and ongoing monitoring after deployment. When vulnerabilities are identified in third party components, organizations must be able to respond quickly to mitigate exposure.

Microsoft cloud platforms support third party risk management through identity controls, access monitoring, and policy enforcement. By integrating these capabilities into governance processes, organizations can maintain oversight without impeding collaboration. Automated alerts and reporting provide early warning of unusual activity associated with external access.

Managing third party and supply chain risk is essential to maintaining trust in cloud ecosystems. It acknowledges that security is not limited to internal controls but extends to the broader network of relationships that support operations. By embedding third party risk management into governance frameworks, organizations strengthen their ability to operate securely in interconnected cloud environments.

These additional governance dimensions reinforce the role of structure, accountability, and visibility in cloud security. When governance is embedded into architecture, operations, and external relationships, it becomes a powerful enabler of resilience. In Microsoft cloud environments, this integrated approach ensures that security remains effective even as systems, partnerships, and threats continue to evolve.

Chapter 8

Incident Response, Recovery, and Business Continuity in the Cloud

Security incidents in cloud environments are inevitable, not because defenses are inadequate, but because modern systems are complex, interconnected, and constantly changing. In Microsoft cloud deployments, where services operate continuously and at scale, the true measure of cyber resilience is revealed not at the point of prevention, but at the moment of response. How an organization detects, contains, recovers from, and continues operating during an incident determines whether disruption remains manageable or escalates into prolonged damage.

Incident response in cloud environments requires a fundamental shift from traditional approaches. In legacy systems, response actions were often linear and manual. Systems were isolated physically, servers were taken offline, and investigations unfolded over extended periods. Microsoft cloud environments operate under different conditions. Resources are virtualized, identities span multiple services, and workloads can be replicated or redeployed rapidly. These characteristics demand response models that are flexible, coordinated, and capable of operating at cloud speed.

Preparation is the cornerstone of effective incident response. Organizations that attempt to design response processes during an active incident often struggle with confusion, delayed decision making, and inconsistent actions. In resilient cloud environments, response roles and responsibilities are defined in advance. Teams understand who is authorized to revoke access, isolate workloads, communicate with stakeholders, and approve recovery actions. This clarity reduces friction during high pressure situations and enables faster containment.

Cloud incidents often involve multiple layers simultaneously. A single event may include identity compromise, network misuse, configuration changes, and data exposure. Effective response requires coordination across security, cloud operations, network teams, and leadership. In Microsoft cloud environments, this coordination is supported by centralized visibility and clearly defined escalation paths. Without coordination, teams may act independently, inadvertently disrupting operations or destroying forensic evidence.

Containment strategies must balance urgency with precision. Immediate action is often required to stop attacker activity, but overly aggressive containment can disrupt legitimate services and complicate recovery. In cloud environments, containment may involve disabling identities, restricting network access, or isolating specific workloads. These actions must be targeted and reversible, allowing organizations to limit impact while preserving operational continuity.

Automation significantly enhances containment capability. Manual intervention is often too slow to address fast moving threats that exploit automation and scale. Automated response workflows enable immediate enforcement of security controls when risk thresholds are exceeded. In Microsoft cloud deployments, automation allows response actions to be executed consistently and logged for accountability. This consistency is essential for both operational effectiveness and compliance.

Recovery is a distinct phase that requires deliberate planning and execution. Once threats are contained, organizations must restore systems to a trusted state. In cloud environments, recovery is not simply about bringing services back online. It involves validating configurations, rotating credentials, reviewing access permissions, and ensuring that vulnerabilities have been addressed. Rushing recovery without proper validation risks reintroducing compromised systems into production.

Data recovery is a critical aspect of this phase. Microsoft cloud environments host data across multiple services and regions. Backup strategies must account for data integrity, retention requirements, and recovery priorities. Resilient organizations define clear recovery objectives that reflect business impact rather than treating all data equally. Regular testing of backup and restoration processes ensures that recovery plans function as intended under real conditions.

Business continuity extends beyond technical recovery. Cyber incidents affect customer trust, regulatory obligations, and organizational reputation. Continuity planning ensures that essential business functions remain available or can be restored quickly during disruption. In cloud driven enterprises, continuity may involve failover to alternate environments, temporary operational workarounds, or staged service restoration. These strategies must be documented, tested, and aligned with overall business priorities.

Microsoft cloud platforms provide capabilities that support continuity through redundancy, geographic distribution, and elastic scaling. However, these capabilities do not guarantee resilience on their own. They must be designed into architectures intentionally and tested regularly. Dependencies between systems, regions, and services must be understood to avoid unexpected failures during incidents.

Communication is a critical but often underestimated component of incident response and continuity. Internal teams need accurate, timely information to coordinate actions effectively. External stakeholders, including customers and regulators, may require updates depending on the nature of the incident. Clear communication plans reduce uncertainty and support trust during disruptive events.

Post incident analysis is essential for continuous improvement. Cloud environments generate extensive logs and telemetry that provide valuable insight into how incidents unfold. Reviewing this information allows organizations to identify gaps in detection, response, and recovery processes. Lessons learned should inform updates to security architecture, automation logic, and governance frameworks.

Incident response, recovery, and business continuity are not isolated activities. They form a continuous cycle that strengthens resilience over time. Each incident provides an opportunity to refine processes, improve coordination, and enhance preparedness. In Microsoft cloud environments, where change is constant, this cycle of learning and adaptation is particularly important.

8.1 Preparing for Cloud Incidents Through Structured Response Planning

Effective incident response in Microsoft cloud environments begins long before an alert is triggered. Preparation is not simply about having a written incident response document. It is about ensuring that people, processes, and technology are aligned to act decisively under pressure. In cloud driven enterprises, where incidents can escalate quickly, unprepared organizations often lose valuable time deciding what to do rather than executing a response.

Structured response planning starts with clearly defined roles and responsibilities. In cloud environments, incident response involves more than the security team alone. Cloud administrators, identity managers, network engineers, application owners, legal teams, and executive leadership may all play a role depending on the nature of the incident. Without predefined responsibilities, response efforts become fragmented, leading to duplicated actions or critical gaps.

Resilient organizations establish clear authority for response actions. Decisions such as disabling accounts, isolating workloads, or modifying network controls must be authorized in advance. In Microsoft cloud environments, where access and configurations can be changed instantly, uncertainty around authority can delay containment. Clear escalation paths ensure that decisions are made quickly and consistently.

Preparation also involves defining incident categories and response priorities. Not all incidents require the same level of response. A suspected credential misuse event demands a different approach from a confirmed data exposure or service disruption. Structured response planning categorizes incidents based on severity, scope, and business impact. This classification guides response actions and ensures that resources are allocated appropriately.

Technical preparation is equally important. Response plans must account for how cloud specific actions are executed. This includes procedures for revoking identity access, isolating cloud resources, preserving logs, and restricting network communication. In Microsoft cloud environments, these actions should be tested regularly to ensure teams are familiar with execution steps and potential side effects.

Training and simulation play a critical role in preparedness. Tabletop exercises and simulated incidents allow teams to practice response workflows without real world consequences. These exercises reveal gaps in communication, unclear responsibilities, and technical limitations. Over time, repeated simulations improve confidence and coordination, reducing hesitation during actual incidents.

Preparedness also extends to documentation and tooling. Response teams must have access to up to date architecture diagrams, asset inventories, and contact information. In cloud environments that change frequently, outdated documentation can hinder response. Resilient organizations treat documentation as a living resource that evolves alongside infrastructure.

Ultimately, structured response planning transforms incident response from an improvised activity into an operational capability. In Microsoft cloud environments, where speed and coordination are critical, preparation determines whether response efforts are controlled and effective or reactive and chaotic.

8.2 Containment Strategies That Balance Speed, Precision, and Continuity

Containment is one of the most critical phases of incident response, yet it is also one of the most challenging. In Microsoft cloud environments, containment actions must be executed quickly to prevent escalation, but they must also be precise to avoid unnecessary disruption. Poorly planned containment can cause as much damage as the incident itself.

Unlike traditional environments, cloud systems are highly interconnected. A single identity may access multiple services, and a single workload may support multiple business processes. Containment strategies must therefore be designed to limit attacker activity without disrupting unrelated operations. Broad actions such as disabling entire networks or shutting down multiple services may stop an attack, but they can also interrupt essential business functions.

Resilient containment strategies prioritize targeted actions. In Microsoft cloud environments, this often involves isolating specific identities, workloads, or network segments rather than entire systems. For example, revoking access for a compromised identity may be sufficient to stop attacker activity without affecting other users. Similarly, isolating a specific virtual machine or application can contain an incident while preserving broader system availability.

Automation plays a key role in achieving this balance. Automated containment workflows can execute predefined actions immediately when risk thresholds are exceeded. These workflows operate faster than manual processes and reduce reliance on human availability during critical moments. However, automation must be governed carefully to prevent unintended consequences.

Effective containment strategies also consider reversibility. Actions taken during containment should be recoverable once the incident is under control. Disabling access, applying restrictive network rules, or suspending services should be logged and documented to support restoration during recovery. In Microsoft cloud environments, where changes can be made rapidly, maintaining a clear record of actions is essential.

Containment decisions must also account for evidence preservation. Overly aggressive actions can destroy logs or disrupt forensic analysis. Resilient response frameworks balance containment with the need to understand how the incident occurred. Preserving identity logs, configuration histories, and network activity supports post incident investigation and long term improvement.

Communication is another critical element during containment. Technical teams must coordinate actions to avoid conflict or duplication. Leadership must be informed of potential business impact, and where necessary, legal or compliance teams may need to be involved. Clear communication protocols reduce confusion and ensure alignment during fast moving situations.

In cloud environments, containment is not a single action but a sequence of decisions. Initial containment may stop immediate threat activity, followed by additional measures as understanding improves. Resilient organizations view containment as an adaptive process that evolves as more information becomes available.

By designing containment strategies that balance speed, precision, and continuity, organizations strengthen their ability to manage incidents effectively. In Microsoft cloud environments, where disruption can spread quickly, this balance is essential to maintaining trust and operational stability.

8.3 Validating Recovery and Restoring Trust After Cloud Incidents

Recovery in Microsoft cloud environments is often misunderstood as the moment systems come back online. In reality, recovery is not complete until trust is restored. Simply restarting services or re enabling access does not guarantee that systems are secure, stable, or free from attacker persistence. Resilient recovery requires deliberate validation to ensure that environments are returned to a known good state.

Cloud incidents frequently involve subtle changes that are not immediately visible. Attackers may modify access permissions, introduce backdoor configurations, or create hidden resources that survive initial containment. Without thorough validation, these remnants can allow attackers to regain access after recovery. Effective recovery therefore focuses on verification rather than speed alone.

Validation begins with identity hygiene. Compromised credentials must be rotated, access permissions reviewed, and privileged roles reassessed. In Microsoft cloud environments, where identities often span multiple services, this process must be comprehensive. Recovery teams must ensure that no unauthorized accounts remain and that privilege assignments reflect least access principles.

Configuration validation is equally important. During incidents, security teams may apply temporary controls such as restrictive network rules or emergency policies. Recovery requires reviewing these changes to determine which should remain and which should be reverted. At the same time, configurations must be assessed for unauthorized modifications introduced during the incident. This includes reviewing resource settings, automation scripts, and deployment templates.

Data integrity validation is a critical component of trust restoration. Even when backups are available, organizations must verify that restored data is accurate, complete, and untampered. In Microsoft cloud environments, where data may be distributed across services and regions, this validation requires coordination between application owners and data teams. Recovery without integrity assurance risks propagating corrupted or compromised data.

Testing plays a central role in validating recovery. Applications and services must be tested under realistic conditions to ensure they behave as expected. Security controls should be exercised to confirm that detection and response mechanisms are functioning correctly. This testing provides confidence that recovery actions have not introduced new vulnerabilities or operational instability.

Communication is an essential aspect of trust restoration. Internal stakeholders need assurance that systems are safe to use, while external stakeholders may require confirmation that risks have been addressed. Transparent communication supported by evidence strengthens confidence and reduces uncertainty following incidents.

Recovery validation also feeds directly into long term resilience. Lessons learned during recovery should inform improvements to architecture, automation, and response planning. In Microsoft cloud environments, where changes can be implemented quickly, recovery insights provide valuable guidance for strengthening defenses against future incidents.

Ultimately, recovery is not just a technical exercise. It is a process of reestablishing confidence in systems, data, and operations. Organizations that prioritize validation over haste are better positioned to sustain trust and stability after cloud security incidents.

8.4 Sustaining Business Continuity During Prolonged Cloud Disruptions

Business continuity planning often focuses on short term outages, yet many cyber incidents involve prolonged disruption rather than immediate failure. In Microsoft cloud environments, incidents may require extended containment, investigation, or staged recovery. During this time, organizations must continue operating despite degraded systems. Sustaining continuity under these conditions is a defining element of cyber resilience.

Continuity planning begins with understanding business priorities. Not all services are equally critical. Organizations must identify which functions are essential to maintain during disruption and which can tolerate delay. In cloud environments, this prioritization informs decisions about resource allocation, recovery sequencing, and communication.

Architectural design plays a significant role in continuity. Microsoft cloud platforms offer capabilities such as geographic redundancy, load distribution, and failover mechanisms. However, these features must be aligned with continuity objectives. Redundancy alone does not guarantee continuity if dependencies are not understood or tested. Resilient organizations map service dependencies and design continuity strategies that account for both technical and operational relationships.

Operational flexibility is another key factor. During prolonged incidents, teams may need to adopt alternative workflows or temporary processes. Business continuity planning ensures that these alternatives are documented and accessible. For example, manual processes may replace automated systems, or secondary platforms may support essential functions. Preparing for these scenarios reduces confusion and maintains productivity during disruption.

Human factors are often overlooked in continuity planning. Extended incidents place significant stress on teams, leading to fatigue and reduced effectiveness. Resilient continuity strategies account for staffing rotation, clear communication, and decision support. Maintaining team well being is essential to sustaining operations over time.

Communication remains critical throughout prolonged disruptions. Stakeholders require regular updates that reflect evolving conditions. Clear, consistent messaging reduces uncertainty and prevents misinformation. In regulated environments, communication may also be subject to legal or regulatory requirements. Continuity planning ensures that communication responsibilities are defined and supported.

Testing continuity plans is essential to their effectiveness. Plans that exist only on paper often fail under real conditions. In Microsoft cloud environments, continuity testing should simulate realistic disruption scenarios, including extended outages or partial system availability. These tests reveal weaknesses and allow organizations to refine strategies before real incidents occur.

Sustaining continuity during prolonged disruption is not about maintaining normal operations. It is about preserving essential functions while managing risk and uncertainty. Organizations that plan for extended disruption are better equipped to adapt and recover without compromising stability or trust.

Chapter 9

Measuring, Testing, and Continuously Improving Cyber Resilience

Cyber resilience is not a static achievement. In Microsoft cloud environments, where architectures evolve and threats adapt continuously, resilience must be measured, tested, and refined over time. Organizations that assume security controls remain effective indefinitely often discover weaknesses only after incidents occur. Measuring and improving resilience requires intentional effort, reliable indicators, and a commitment to learning from both success and failure.

Measurement provides visibility into how well security controls perform under real conditions. In cloud environments, traditional metrics such as compliance status or tool deployment offer limited insight. Resilience measurement focuses on outcomes rather than presence. It examines how quickly threats are detected, how effectively incidents are contained, and how reliably systems recover. These indicators reflect the true ability of an organization to withstand and adapt to disruption.

Testing plays a critical role in validating resilience. Assumptions about security effectiveness are often unchallenged until an incident exposes gaps. Regular testing allows organizations to identify weaknesses before attackers do. In Microsoft cloud environments, testing includes simulating identity compromise, network misuse, configuration errors, and service disruption. These exercises reveal how controls behave in practice rather than in theory.

Continuous improvement links measurement and testing to action. Metrics and test results must inform changes to architecture, processes, and automation. Without follow through, measurement becomes an academic exercise rather than a driver of resilience. Resilient organizations treat every test and incident as an opportunity to refine their defenses and improve response capability.

One challenge in measuring cloud resilience is selecting meaningful indicators. Metrics should align with organizational objectives and risk tolerance. Measuring too many indicators creates noise, while measuring too few hides critical weaknesses. Effective resilience measurement focuses on indicators that reflect detection speed, response accuracy, recovery reliability, and continuity effectiveness.

Microsoft cloud environments generate extensive telemetry that supports resilience measurement. Logs, alerts, configuration data, and response records provide insight into system behavior and control performance. Resilient organizations integrate this data into dashboards and reporting mechanisms that support decision making at both technical and executive levels.

Testing strategies must reflect the complexity of cloud environments. Simple checks are insufficient to capture the interactions between identities, networks, automation, and governance. Comprehensive testing involves coordinated scenarios that span multiple layers. These scenarios should reflect realistic threat behavior and operational constraints.

Continuous improvement requires cultural alignment as well as technical capability. Teams must be willing to acknowledge weaknesses and prioritize improvement over blame. Governance frameworks support this culture by defining expectations for testing, review, and remediation. Leadership engagement reinforces the importance of resilience as an ongoing objective rather than a one-time project.

Automation enhances the ability to test and improve resilience at scale. Automated testing and validation processes can evaluate control effectiveness continuously, reducing reliance on periodic exercises. In Microsoft cloud environments, automation allows resilience improvement to keep pace with infrastructure change.

9.1 Defining Meaningful Resilience Metrics Beyond Compliance and Tool Adoption

Measuring cyber resilience in Microsoft cloud environments requires moving beyond traditional indicators that focus on tool deployment or compliance status. Many organizations assume that passing audits or implementing security platforms equates to resilience. In reality, these indicators reveal very little about how systems behave when faced with real world disruption. Resilience metrics must evaluate capability under pressure, not preparedness on paper.

Meaningful resilience measurement begins by identifying outcomes rather than activities. Instead of asking whether monitoring tools are enabled, organizations must ask how quickly suspicious behavior is identified once it occurs. In cloud environments, where attackers can exploit automation and scale, detection speed is a critical indicator. Measuring time to detect identity misuse, abnormal access patterns, or configuration drift provides insight into whether monitoring and analytics are truly effective.

Detection metrics alone are insufficient without understanding accuracy. Excessive alerts can give the impression of strong monitoring while overwhelming security teams and obscuring genuine threats. Resilient measurement frameworks therefore assess signal quality alongside speed. Metrics such as false positive rates, alert correlation effectiveness, and analyst escalation accuracy reveal whether detection systems produce actionable intelligence rather than noise.

Response metrics add another layer of insight. Once a threat is detected, organizations must evaluate how quickly and precisely they respond. Time to contain is a key indicator, but it must be interpreted carefully. Rapid containment that disrupts critical services may indicate poor response design rather than strength. Resilient metrics examine containment scope, service impact, and reversibility of actions to determine whether response strategies are balanced and effective.

Recovery metrics complete the resilience picture. Organizations should measure how reliably systems return to a trusted state after incidents. This includes evaluating recovery time against defined objectives, validating configuration integrity, and confirming data accuracy. Repeated recovery delays or inconsistencies often indicate deeper architectural or process weaknesses that require attention.

Contextual interpretation is essential for all resilience metrics. Numbers without narrative can mislead decision makers. For example, improved detection times may coincide with increased alert volume during detection tuning. Resilient measurement frameworks pair quantitative metrics with qualitative analysis to ensure that improvements reflect real capability rather than temporary fluctuation.

Ultimately, defining meaningful resilience metrics enables organizations to understand their true defensive posture. In Microsoft cloud environments, where complexity and change are constant, these metrics provide a clear lens through which resilience can be assessed, communicated, and improved over time.

9.2 Stress Testing Cloud Security Through Continuous, Coordinated, and Realistic Validation

Assumptions about security effectiveness are among the most dangerous risks in cloud environments. Controls that appear strong under normal conditions may fail under coordinated attack or operational stress. Stress testing provides a way to challenge these assumptions before attackers do. In Microsoft cloud deployments, effective testing must reflect the interconnected and dynamic nature of modern systems.

Scenario based testing forms the foundation of realistic validation. Rather than testing isolated controls, organizations simulate complete attack paths that span identity compromise, network movement, automation misuse, and governance failure. These scenarios mirror how real attackers operate and reveal weaknesses that component level tests cannot detect. For example, a credential compromise scenario may expose delays in detection, gaps in network containment, or confusion around response authority.

Continuous validation complements scenario based exercises by assessing controls as environments evolve. Cloud deployments change constantly as new resources are added and configurations modified. Without continuous testing, resilience can degrade silently. Automated validation checks ensure that security baselines remain intact and that drift is detected early. This approach shifts testing from a periodic activity to an ongoing discipline.

Human response capability must also be tested. Incident response involves judgment, coordination, and communication under pressure. Tabletop exercises and live simulations allow teams to practice decision making and collaboration without real world consequences. These exercises often reveal non-technical weaknesses such as unclear escalation paths, delayed approvals, or communication breakdowns that can significantly impact response effectiveness.

Testing must include failure conditions. Many resilience gaps emerge only when systems behave unexpectedly. Simulating partial outages, delayed alerts, or unavailable dependencies helps organizations understand how response and recovery plans perform under stress. In Microsoft cloud environments, where dependencies can be complex, this type of testing is essential.

Testing programs must evolve alongside threat landscapes and architectures. Scenarios that were relevant a year ago may no longer reflect current risk. Resilient organizations update testing strategies regularly to address new services, integrations, and attack techniques. This adaptability ensures that testing remains relevant and valuable.

Through continuous and coordinated testing, organizations gain confidence in their ability to withstand disruption. Rather than relying on assumptions, they validate resilience through experience, strengthening preparedness and response capability over time.

9.3 Institutionalizing Continuous Improvement as a Core Resilience Capability

Measurement and testing are valuable only when they lead to sustained improvement. Continuous improvement is the mechanism that transforms insights into lasting resilience. In Microsoft cloud environments, where change is constant, improvement must be embedded into governance, operations, and culture to remain effective.

Continuous improvement begins with disciplined review processes. After incidents, tests, or near misses, organizations must analyze outcomes systematically. These reviews examine detection performance, response decisions, recovery effectiveness, and communication outcomes. The goal is not to assign blame but to understand systemic weaknesses and opportunities for enhancement.

Improvement initiatives often span multiple domains. A single incident may reveal architectural weaknesses, automation gaps, and governance misalignment simultaneously. Resilient organizations address these issues holistically rather than in isolation. Improvements are prioritized based on risk and impact, ensuring that resources are directed where they matter most.

Automation accelerates improvement by enabling rapid deployment of changes. In Microsoft cloud environments, configurations, policies, and workflows can be updated programmatically. This agility allows organizations to close gaps quickly and validate fixes through testing. Continuous improvement cycles shorten as feedback loops tighten.

Governance frameworks play a critical role in sustaining improvement. Policies define expectations for review frequency, remediation timelines, and accountability. Without governance, improvement efforts often stall due to competing priorities. Clear ownership ensures that identified issues are addressed rather than deferred indefinitely.

Cultural factors are equally important. Continuous improvement requires openness to critique and willingness to adapt. Teams must feel supported in reporting weaknesses and proposing changes. Leadership commitment reinforces this culture by prioritizing resilience alongside delivery and innovation.

Over time, continuous improvement becomes a defining organizational capability. Security programs evolve proactively rather than reactively. Lessons from incidents and tests strengthen architecture, refine automation, and improve coordination. In cloud environments, where threats and technologies evolve rapidly, this adaptability is the foundation of long term cyber resilience.

Chapter 10

The Future of Cloud and Network Cyber Resilience

Cyber resilience is no longer defined by how well organizations defend against known threats. It is defined by how effectively they adapt to uncertainty. In Microsoft cloud environments, where technology evolves faster than policy and attackers innovate faster than controls, the future of resilience depends on anticipation, adaptability, and disciplined execution rather than static protection models.

The cloud has fundamentally altered the security landscape. Infrastructure is programmable, identities are fluid, and services are deeply interconnected across networks, regions, and organizations. These characteristics will only intensify as enterprises continue to adopt distributed architectures, integrate artificial intelligence into operations, and rely more heavily on automation. The future of cyber resilience lies in embracing these realities rather than attempting to control them through legacy approaches.

One of the most significant shifts shaping the future is the move from reactive security to predictive resilience. Traditional security models respond to events after they occur. Resilient cloud environments increasingly rely on predictive signals that indicate elevated risk before damage is done. Behavioral trends, configuration drift patterns, and identity anomalies provide early warning that systems are approaching failure conditions. Organizations that learn to interpret and act on these signals will reduce incident frequency and impact significantly.

Artificial intelligence will play an expanding role in this evolution. As cloud environments grow in scale and complexity, human driven analysis alone will not be sufficient. AI will increasingly support risk forecasting, automated control adjustment, and decision support during incidents. However, the future does not belong to automation without oversight. Resilience depends on combining machine speed with human judgment. Organizations that treat AI as an assistant rather than an authority will be better positioned to manage risk responsibly.

Another defining trend is the continued convergence of identity, network, and application security. In future cloud environments, these domains will no longer operate as separate layers. Identity will increasingly determine network access. Application behavior will influence trust decisions. Network signals will inform identity risk scoring. This convergence will enable more precise control and faster response, but it will also demand tighter coordination across teams and disciplines.

Hybrid and multi cloud environments will remain a reality for most organizations. Complete migration to a single platform is rarely feasible due to regulatory, operational, and strategic constraints. The future of resilience therefore depends on designing security frameworks that operate consistently across environments rather than optimizing for a single platform. Microsoft cloud environments will continue to coexist with on premise systems and third party services, making interoperability and unified governance essential.

Governance itself will evolve from oversight to enablement. As cloud operations accelerate, governance models that rely on manual approval and retrospective review will struggle to remain relevant. Future governance frameworks will be embedded directly into architecture and automation, guiding decisions in real time. These frameworks will define acceptable risk boundaries while allowing teams to innovate within them. Organizations that strike this balance will maintain both agility and control.

Regulatory expectations will also shape the future of resilience. As cloud adoption becomes universal, regulators are increasingly focused on operational resilience rather than technical compliance alone. Demonstrating the ability to detect, respond to, and recover from incidents will become as important as meeting control requirements. Organizations that invest in resilience measurement, testing, and continuous improvement will be better prepared to meet these expectations.

Human factors will remain central to resilience despite technological advances. Skills development, cross functional collaboration, and leadership commitment will determine whether resilience strategies succeed or fail. The future of cloud security will demand professionals who understand not only tools and platforms, but also systems thinking and risk tradeoffs. Building and retaining this capability will be a strategic priority for resilient organizations.

Cultural maturity will increasingly differentiate resilient enterprises from vulnerable ones. Organizations that view incidents as failures to be hidden will repeat mistakes. Those that treat incidents as learning opportunities will strengthen over time. Transparency, accountability, and continuous improvement will define resilience culture in the cloud era.

Looking forward, cyber resilience will not be achieved through a single architecture, framework, or technology. It will be achieved through disciplined integration of identity, network defense, automation, governance, and human judgment. Microsoft cloud environments provide powerful capabilities to support this integration, but capability alone does not guarantee resilience. Intentional design, consistent execution, and continuous learning are required.

10.1 Emerging Technologies and the Evolution of Adaptive Cloud Defense

The future of cloud and network cyber resilience will be shaped heavily by emerging technologies that change how systems are built, monitored, and defended. As Microsoft cloud environments continue to integrate advanced capabilities such as artificial intelligence, serverless computing, edge services, and autonomous automation, security models must evolve in parallel. Static defenses designed for predictable systems will struggle to remain effective in environments that are increasingly self-configuring and event driven.

One major shift will be the rise of adaptive security controls that adjust dynamically based on real time risk. Instead of relying on fixed policies, future cloud defenses will continuously recalibrate trust decisions using behavioral signals, environmental context, and historical patterns. For example, access privileges may fluctuate based on recent activity, device posture, or detected anomalies rather than remaining permanently assigned. This adaptability reduces exposure windows and limits attacker persistence.

AI driven systems will increasingly support decision making at both tactical and strategic levels. In Microsoft cloud environments, machine learning models will help forecast potential failure points by analyzing trends such as gradual permission creep, recurring misconfigurations, or abnormal automation behavior. These insights allow organizations to address weaknesses before they are exploited. However, reliance on predictive systems also introduces new risks related to model accuracy, bias, and explainability. Resilient organizations will invest in transparency and validation to ensure that automated insights are trusted and understood.

Edge computing and distributed workloads will further complicate defense strategies. As processing moves closer to users and devices, traditional centralized monitoring becomes less effective. Future resilience frameworks must account for decentralized visibility and enforcement. Security controls will need to operate consistently across core cloud platforms, edge locations, and connected devices. This expansion of scope requires unified identity governance and standardized telemetry to maintain situational awareness.

Another emerging factor is the growing reliance on automation and infrastructure as code. While automation improves efficiency and consistency, it also amplifies the impact of errors. A single flawed template can introduce systemic vulnerabilities across environments. Future resilience strategies will place greater emphasis on validating automation pipelines, enforcing policy controls during deployment, and continuously testing infrastructure changes. In this context, resilience depends not only on defending running systems but also on securing the processes that create them.

As these technologies mature, the boundary between operations and security will continue to blur. Security controls will increasingly be embedded directly into application logic, deployment workflows, and operational tooling. This integration reflects a broader trend toward treating security as an inherent system property rather than an external layer. Organizations that adapt to this paradigm will be better equipped to manage complexity and uncertainty in evolving cloud ecosystems.

10.2 Strategic Leadership and Long Term Resilience in Cloud Centric Enterprises

While technology will drive much of the evolution in cloud security, long term resilience ultimately depends on strategic leadership. Decisions about architecture, risk tolerance, investment, and culture shape how effectively organizations adapt to disruption. In Microsoft cloud environments, where security choices have enterprise wide implications, leadership engagement is a defining factor in resilience maturity.

Strategic leaders play a critical role in aligning resilience objectives with business priorities. Cyber resilience is often framed as a technical issue, but its impact extends to service availability, customer trust, regulatory standing, and organizational reputation. Leaders who understand these connections are better positioned to support security initiatives that may not deliver immediate visible returns but provide long term stability.

Investment decisions will increasingly reflect this perspective. Rather than focusing solely on preventive controls, resilient organizations allocate resources to detection, response, recovery, and continuous improvement. This balanced investment acknowledges that prevention alone cannot eliminate risk. Leadership commitment ensures that resilience capabilities are funded, maintained, and prioritized even in the absence of major incidents.

Leadership also influences how organizations respond to failure. In resilient enterprises, incidents are treated as learning opportunities rather than sources of blame. Post incident reviews are supported at the highest levels, and lessons learned are translated into tangible improvements. This approach fosters transparency and continuous improvement, strengthening resilience over time.

Talent development is another strategic concern. The future of cloud resilience requires professionals who can navigate technical complexity while understanding business context. Leaders must invest in training, cross functional collaboration, and career pathways that encourage systems thinking. Building this capability internally reduces dependence on reactive external support and strengthens organizational autonomy.

Governance frameworks reflect leadership values as well. Leaders who prioritize clarity and accountability create environments where security responsibilities are understood and enforced. In Microsoft cloud environments, this clarity supports consistent decision making and faster response during incidents. Governance becomes a strategic asset rather than an administrative burden.

Ultimately, the future of cloud and network cyber resilience will be shaped as much by leadership choices as by technological innovation. Organizations that treat resilience as a strategic discipline embedded into planning, culture, and execution will adapt more effectively to uncertainty. Those that view it as a technical afterthought will struggle as complexity and risk continue to grow.

Reviews

1. Dr. Kabiru Mustapha Adekunle, Senior Lecturer in Cybersecurity Studies

This book demonstrates a strong command of both academic research and applied security practice. The examination of Microsoft cloud security and network defense is detailed, methodical, and supported by credible scholarly sources. The focus on cyber resilience as a sustained operational capability makes this work particularly relevant for modern enterprises.

2. Engr. Morenike Adebisi Falade, Cloud Infrastructure and Systems Architect

Pioneers of Cyber Resilience provides a clear and practical understanding of how secure cloud environments should be designed and managed. The discussion of Microsoft Azure and hybrid network security reflects real deployment challenges faced by organizations today.

3. Abdulrahman Sulaiman Lawani, Director of Security Operations

This book stands out for its emphasis on resilience as a continuous security objective. The treatment of AI enabled automation, threat detection, and governance aligns closely with the realities of enterprise security operations. The research is solid, and the insights are directly applicable to both strategic planning and operational execution

4. Dr. Halima Rukayat Danjuma, Compliance and Risk Management Specialist

The integration of governance frameworks with cloud security implementation is handled with notable precision. The discussion of ISO 27001 and NIST standards demonstrates how regulatory requirements can be embedded into Microsoft cloud environments without creating operational friction.

5. Ifeanyi Chukwuma Ezenwa, Network and Cloud Defense Engineer

This work adopts a comprehensive approach to modern cybersecurity challenges. By connecting cloud architecture, network defense, artificial intelligence, and incident response, it reflects how security functions in complex, real world environments. The technical depth is balanced with strategic insight, giving the book lasting relevance for practitioners and decision makers alike.

References

Behl, A., & Behl, K. (2017). Cyberwar: The next threat to national security and what to do about it. Oxford University Press.

Behl, A., & Greatbanks, R. (2016). Cybersecurity and cyberwar: What everyone needs to know. Oxford University Press.

Cichonski, P., Millar, T., Grance, T., & Scarfone, K. (2012). Computer security incident handling guide (NIST Special Publication 800-61 Rev. 2). National Institute of Standards and Technology. https://doi.org/10.6028/NIST.SP.800-61r2

ENISA. (2023). Threat landscape 2023. European Union Agency for Cybersecurity. https://www.enisa.europa.eu/publications/enisa-threat-landscape-2023

Gartner. (2023). Predicts 2025: Cybersecurity. Gartner Research.

ISO/IEC. (2022). ISO/IEC 27001:2022 information security, cybersecurity and privacy protection — Information security management systems — Requirements. International Organization for Standardization.

Kindervag, J. (2010). Build security into your network's DNA: The zero trust network architecture. Forrester Research.

Kshetri, N. (2021). Cybersecurity management: An organizational and strategic approach. University of Toronto Press. https://doi.org/10.3138/9781487538645

Microsoft. (2023). Microsoft Azure security best practices. https://learn.microsoft.com/en-us/azure/security/fundamentals/best-practices-and-patterns

Microsoft. (2024). Zero Trust guidance for Azure and hybrid environments. https://learn.microsoft.com/en-us/security/zero-trust/

NIST. (2018). Framework for improving critical infrastructure cybersecurity (Version 1.1). National Institute of Standards and Technology. https://doi.org/10.6028/NIST.CSWP.04162018

NIST. (2020). Security and privacy controls for information systems and organizations (Special Publication 800-53 Rev. 5). National Institute of Standards and Technology. https://doi.org/10.6028/NIST.SP.800-53r5

NIST. (2023). Artificial intelligence risk management framework (AI RMF 1.0). National Institute of Standards and Technology. https://doi.org/10.6028/NIST.AI.100-1

Ponemon Institute. (2023). Cost of a data breach report 2023. IBM Security. https://www.ibm.com/security/data-breach

Scarfone, K., & Souppaya, M. (2022). Guide to zero trust architecture (NIST Special Publication 800-207). National Institute of Standards and Technology. https://doi.org/10.6028/NIST.SP.800-207

Shackelford, S. J. (2020). Managing cyber attacks in international law, business, and relations. Cambridge University Press. https://doi.org/10.1017/9781108591714

Sommer, R., & Paxson, V. (2010). Outside the closed world: On using machine learning for network intrusion detection. IEEE Symposium on Security and Privacy, 305–316. https://doi.org/10.1109/SP.2010.25

Stallings, W., & Brown, L. (2018). Computer security: Principles and practice (4th ed.). Pearson Education.

Taleb, N. N. (2012). Antifragile: Things that gain from disorder. Random House.

Verizon. (2024). Data breach investigations report. Verizon Enterprise Solutions. https://www.verizon.com/business/resources/reports/dbir/

Wulf, W. A., & Jones, A. K. (2021). Cyber resilience engineering: Concepts and practice. IEEE Security & Privacy, 19(4), 62–70. https://doi.org/10.1109/MSEC.2021.3072303

www.ingramcontent.com/pod-product-compliance
Lightning Source LLC
Chambersburg PA
CBHW021214250926
51852CB00006B/9
9787755254728